Cavan, 1609–1653

Maynooth Studies in Local History

SERIES EDITOR Raymond Gillespie

This volume is one of five short books published in the Maynooth Studies in Local History series in 2007. Like their predecessors their aim is to explore aspects of the local experience of the Irish past. That local experience is not a simple chronicling of events that took place within a narrow set of administrative or geographically determined boundaries. Rather the local experience in the past encompasses all aspects of how local communities of people functioned from birth to death and from the pinnacle of the social order to its base. The study of the local past is as much about the recreation of mental worlds as about the reconstruction of physical ones. It tries to explore motives and meanings as well as the material context for people's beliefs. What held social groups together and what drove them apart are of equal interest and how consensus was achieved and differences managed can help to lay bare the lineaments of the local experience. The subject matter of these short books ranges widely. In the fraught world of the seventeenth century, in which religious division was endemic, communities in Cavan and Strabane managed to find enough common ground to make local worlds workable. Again in nineteenth-century County Dublin the desire for local improvement was sufficient to make the local government system triumph over political and religious division. Distress and division of another kind is evident in the emigration from nineteenth-century Ireland but the return of migrants with wealth and new experiences, an aspect of migration not much studied in the Irish context, helped to bind communities together again. Even in eighteenth-century Edenderry, on the Downshire estate, economic distress and political ferment in the 1790s strangely failed to produce military activity in the area in 1798. Understanding the common assumptions that held these communities together despite the tremendous pressures to which they were subjected is best done at the local level. Such communities remain the key to reconstructing how people, at many spatial and social levels, lived their lives in the past. Such research is at the forefront of Irish historical scholarship and these short books, together with the earlier titles in the series, represent some of the most innovative and exciting work being done in Irish history today. They provide models that others can use and adapt in their own studies of the local past. If these short books convey something of the enthusiasm and excitement that such studies can generate then they will have done their work well.

Maynooth Studies in Local History: Number 71

Cavan, 1609–1653
Plantation, war and religion

Brendan Scott

FOUR COURTS PRESS

Set in 10pt on 12pt Bembo by
Carrigboy Typesetting Services for
FOUR COURTS PRESS LTD
7 Malpas Street, Dublin 8, Ireland
e-mail: info@fourcourtspress.ie
http://www.fourcourtspress.ie
and in North America for
FOUR COURTS PRESS
c/o ISBS, 920 N.E. 58th Avenue, Suite 300, Portland, OR 97213.

ISBN 978–1–84682–062–5

Printed in Ireland
by ßetaprint, Dublin.

Contents

Acknowledgments

While engaged on this project, I have become indebted to a number of people who made its completion a much easier undertaking. I wish to thank the series editor, Professor Raymond Gillespie, for allowing me to present my work as part of the Maynooth local history series. My gratitude is also due to Professor Christopher Maginn for his comments on an earlier draft of this book. My thanks must also go to Savina Donohoe at Cavan County Museum and Tom Sullivan of the Cavan County Library, for all of their help and support. Stephen Hannon of the Geography department at University College Dublin supplied the map of Co. Cavan, for which I am very grateful. The deposition of Richard Bennett is reproduced with the permission of the board of Trinity College Dublin, and the maps of Cavan town, c.1591 and the barony of Loughtee are reproduced courtesy of the National Archives, London.

I wish to thank Fr Liam Kelly for lending me many books of his for months on end and for the many conversations we had on 17th-century Cavan. As can be discerned from a cursory glance at this book's references, much of its secondary material is drawn from the pages of *Breifne*. I wish to pay tribute to those scholars, particularly Bishop Francis MacKiernan and Dr Philip O'Connell, who have ploughed this furrow before me, allowing for easier access into this period of our history.

I also wish to thank my parents John and Rose, my sister Sinead and my brother Martin, for their constant support and interest. I am lucky to have such a kind and generous family. I would also like to thank my nieces Aoise and Annarose, for reminding me that it is much more preferable to live in the present than the past. Finally, my greatest debt is to Tara McGovern, who has supported me always, and it is to her that I dedicate this book.

CONVENTIONS

The year has been taken to begin on 1 January rather than on 25 March, which was the custom of the time.

Unless otherwise stated, all currency is given in Irish valuations.

Introduction

This book deals with Co. Cavan from the opening decade of the 17th century up to the time of the Cromwellian conquest of the county which was completed in 1653. In 1600, Cavan was a border region between the heartlands of Gaelic Ulster and the Anglo-Irish world of the Pale. It had only been recently shired in 1579. Before this, the county was known as the 'Brenny', or 'O'Reilly's country'. As part of a 'surrender and regrant' style policy, Seán O'Reilly, chief of the O'Reillys since 1583, surrendered his lands in exchange for generous terms granted by Lord Deputy John Perrot.[1] Cavan's location as a marcher area buffering the Pale and Gaelic Ulster and bounded by three provinces made it an important strategic point for military forces in Ireland, often drawing the people of Cavan into disputes that were not their immediate concern. Indeed, their proximity to the Pale made them easy prey for raids. One of the reasons why Cavan was shired was in an attempt to control the region.[2] Indeed, Cavan was one of the areas where this tactic met with some measure of success; Aodh Conallach O'Reilly was described in 1581 by the president of Connacht, Sir Nicholas Malby, as 'the best Irish subject in the land', and Archbishop Long of Armagh noted in 1586 the enthusiasm with which the people of Cavan embraced English law and customs.[3] As a result of the Maguire rebellion of 1593, a precursor to the Nine Years War, crown forces, massed in Cavan town, with the agreement of Sir John O'Reilly, launched an attack upon Maguire's stronghold of Enniskillen. This now meant that Cavan would bear the brunt of Maguire's men and sure enough, in February 1595, Maguire razed Cavan town to the ground and wasted most of the county.[4] Following this attack, Cavan fell into a number of years of political instability and violence. John O'Reilly was succeeded by his brother Pilib, who died at the hands of supporters of Hugh O'Neill. Émonn O'Reilly, 90 years old, became chief of the O'Reillys with the help of O'Neill, expelled the small English garrison from Cavan town and raided the Pale, reaching as far as Kells, burning and ravaging as they travelled.[5]

This violence convinced the new viceroy of Ireland, Sir Thomas Burgh, that the subjugation of Cavan and the O'Reillys warranted immediate attention. In February 1597, Burgh and Maol Mórdha O'Reilly, the son of Sir John and current *tánaiste* of the O'Reillys, recaptured the smouldering ruins of Cavan town and installed Maol Mórdha as military commander in the county.[6] Attacks made by O'Neill on Cavan were successfully repulsed.

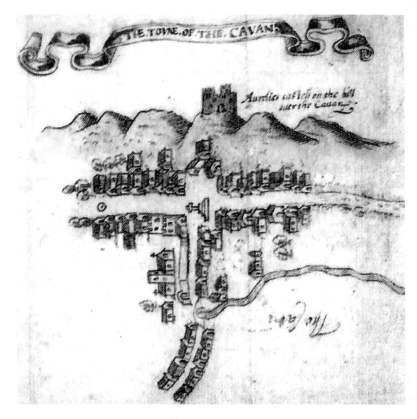

1 Cavan town, *c.*1591

Maol Mórdha died, however, at the battle of the Yellow Ford in August 1598, leaving Émonn free to return to Cavan as chief of the O'Reillys. O'Neill had little confidence in Émonn as a ruler, however, occupying the lordship himself in 1599 and nominating Émonn's nephew, Turlogh Mac Shane O'Reilly, as *tánaiste*. But by the end of that year, there were 1,000 footmen and 100 horsemen garrisoned in Cavan town, under orders to prevent the Irish from joining forces with O'Neill.[7] Lord Mountjoy, the new deputy, had Turlogh executed in 1600, leading O'Neill to nominate Eoghan, Sir John's brother, as the new *tánaiste*. But Émonn had grown tired of O'Neill's interventions in the county, and resisted Eoghan's appointment, a stance backed up by other members of the O'Reilly elite, which led to further civil war in the county.

Mountjoy was not slow to espy an opportunity to exploit the disagreements in Cavan, and sent Conor Maguire, the crown's nominee to the lordship of Fermanagh, and the baron of Dunsany to Cavan, where they set up at Cavan town and Liscannon respectively. With ruthless efficiency, Maguire and Dunsany systematically burned crops and killed livestock, 'leaving neither man nor cattle in the country'.[8] Émonn, forced by the encroachment of Maguire and Dunsany to retreat to the borders of Fermanagh, died in 1601. However, Dunsany, frustrated by his lack of financial gain in the venture, surrendered his fort in Liscannon to Eoghan O'Reilly, a surprise move made all the greater by Eoghan, previously a supporter of O'Neill, suing for peace in 1602 in the wake of the battle of Kinsale. Eoghan died that same year, and a force of 50 men was reckoned to be sufficient to hold Cavan in the name of the crown, a small figure which demonstrates how total Cavan's destruction and subjugation had been.[9]

Cavan, once a bustling and prosperous market town, was now a derelict wreck. The previous seven years of civil war and turmoil had made a huge, and negative, impact upon the county, with many reports of the destruction of livestock and crops, along with the resulting starvation of the people there. Nor had the ruling families escaped lightly; of nine sons born to Aodh Conallach O'Reilly, chief from 1566 to 1583, only four are known to have survived these tumultuous years.[10]

Thus, the conditions within the weakened county were ideal for reorganization. There was no longer anyone within the ruling elite powerful enough to oppose such a move, and many of the county's strongest men had either been killed or had fled the region during the vicious fighting within and without the county, creating a political vacuum which was ready to be filled by a new elite. With this in mind, Lord Deputy Chichester and Attorney General Sir John Davies, along with others, spent a week in Cavan in the summer of 1606, which they described as 'a poor town ... seated betwixt many small hills'.[11] While there, the surveyors satisfied themselves that all of the land in Cavan had been escheated to the crown as a result of the recent rebellion in the area. This made it available for plantation, which Davies was interesting in securing in the area. Following their time in Ulster that summer, Davies was convinced of the Dublin government's impending success against Gaelic law and custom, and foresaw a time when 'every man ... shall know the extent of his estate, whereby the people will be encouraged to manure their land with better industry than heretofore hath been used [and] to bring up their children more civilly'.[12] The only way that this could be done, however, was by introducing a new British settler population to spread ideas of 'civility'. How they administered the plantation in Cavan, the first county in which it was attempted, was vitally important, as it would set a precedent for the future. The conciliatory nature of Davies' negotiations with the people of Cavan had disappeared, to be replaced by something more patronizing and impatient. He refused to listen to the claims made by the native Irish, who, as bordering the Pale, knew something of English law of their 'freehold and of estates of inheritance'. Davies instead claimed the land for James I and lectured the Irish on the civilizing aspect of the plantation process. Now, they would learn to 'build houses, [and] make townships'. Left confused by the legal jargon which Davies used to dazzle them with, the natives, although unhappy with these developments, felt that they had little choice but to give way to the first wave of settlers who would be arriving shortly.[13] The plantation of Ulster had begun.

1. Plantation in Cavan, 1609–41

The plantation in Ulster wrought huge changes in the province.[1] On 4 September 1607, some Ulster lords, including O'Neill and O'Donnell and their supporters, left Ireland for the continent without royal permission. With this action, the lords had renounced their allegiance to King James I. As a result, their lands were escheated to the crown. In January 1608, a plan for this land was published which involved a plantation process akin to that previously attempted in Munster. It was decided that these lands, which comprised the modern counties of Armagh, Cavan, Donegal, Fermanagh, Derry and Tyrone, would be granted to the following groups: Scottish and English undertakers, royal officials known as servitors, the Church of Ireland, schools and the 'deserving' Irish. These 'deserving' Irish were to be existing landholders who were allowed to retain their status on condition that they provided proper, that is, English, leases for their tenants and adopted English styles of dwelling and methods of farming. They also tended to receive the poorest land in Cavan.[2] The plantation was a useful means for the crown to reward cheaply those who had been faithful to the king. Because King James I was Scottish, many of the settlers who were introduced into Ulster were from his native country and Protestant. Thus, the most Gaelic and Catholic province in Ireland became, in theory, the most British and Protestant at a stroke.

The settlers, servitors and 'deserving' Irish were to be granted estates which ranged in size from 1000 to 2000 acres. The settler landlords were to introduce English and Scottish tenants onto the estates and improve their areas through the construction of towns. In 1610, Co. Coleraine was exempted from the scheme; the settlement there was to be carried out by a group of London business companies and as a result the name of the county was changed to Londonderry. In the short term, however, the plantation did not have the impact hoped for by the government. Settlers did not arrive in their expected numbers and the poor social backgrounds of some of the landlords meant that they had difficulty raising the money needed to improve their estates. Moreover, surveys into the plantation held in 1611, 1614, 1619 and 1622 indicated that the settlers were neither fulfilling their building obligations, nor removing the native Irish from their lands as required. Although the articles of plantation required settlers to live in towns or villages, more than two-thirds of the plantation estates contained neither. Many of the undertakers arrived to find more land than they had bargained

2 Barony of Loughtee, 1609

for. Even when villages were built, many other British tenants lived elsewhere on the estate, with many villages only making up between five and twelve houses. Most of the plantation settlers did not live in nucleated settlements of any kind, but were scattered among the townlands they leased and farmed, a situation permitted by the undertakers. It also took over fifteen years for some of the undertakers to provide churches for the new Protestant population. Likewise, many of the schools which were supposed to be provided for the planter's children had not been built by 1622 as required.

It was decided as part of the plantation process that the English and Scottish undertakers in Ulster were to have one and a half times the amount of land allocated to the native Irish. Only the barony of Loughtee was assigned to English undertakers; Scottish undertakers received the baronies of Tullyhunco and Clankee, with the remaining baronies of Tullyhaw, Tullygarvey, Castlerahan and Clanmahon being distributed among servitors and native Irish.³ Indeed, the native Irish received 94,000 acres of land in the province of Ulster, more than the total granted to the English or Scottish settlers or the established church.⁴ As part of the 'Bodley survey', each barony in Cavan was surveyed, maps were made and varying acreage was made available from each for plantation.⁵

Barony	acreage
Loughtee	12,000
Tullyhunco	6,000
Clonkee	6,000
Tullyhaw	9,000
Castlerahan	9,000
Clanmahon	7,000
Tullygarvey	7,500

Source: Hill, *An historical account of the plantation in Ulster*, p. 185.

3 Acres planted in the baronies of Cavan

The major towns planted in the county were Cavan, Virginia and Belturbet. Other smaller settlements included Killeshandra and Ballyhaise. Some of the towns in the plantation process across Ulster, such as Belturbet and Cavan, were to be developed from previous Gaelic settlements; others, such as Virginia, were to be completely new settlements.[6] It was proposed that Virginia be erected 'in or neere the mydwaie between Kells and the Cavan'.[7] Captain John Ridgeway became patron of the area in August 1612.

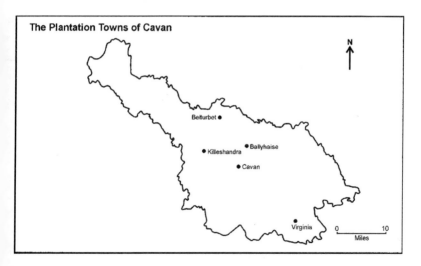

4 Plantation towns of Cavan

As patron, Ridgeway was required to provide land for the town, a church, a market and a school, but he had sold his stake to Captain Hugh Culme by 1619, having failed to build anything of consequence in the area. Nor had Ridgeway attracted 20 residents to the area as required.[8] Ridgeway had, however, brought timber and lime from Fermanagh, Belturbet and Meath for building purposes. To this end, he had demolished five Irish houses near his castle and had arranged for a boat to be built for him at Belturbet for use on Lough Ramor.[9] Hugh Culme was a more conscientious planter than his predecessor, however, and by the time of the 1619 survey, had erected eight timber houses for his English tenants. He had also erected a school and had provided a preacher, probably his brother, Benjamin, for the people in Virginia.[10] Yet his scheme moved at a lacklustre pace, and only five stone and clay houses with poor families were reported by 1622, although two more houses were then under construction.[11] Even these houses were the source of rancour, however. Those building the houses had no assurance that they would be compensated with estates for their troubles, so refused to finish their work until Culme returned from a trip to England, 'for want whereof the poor inhabitants complain'.[12] Culme, whose wife and children were living in the area at the time of the 1622 survey, had built a bawne of stone and lime, within which were two houses made of stone, one three stories high, the other, one and a half. Around the bawne were planted four British families, one of whom kept 'a good Inne' in the area.[13]

Cavan town was also planted during this period. The process was perhaps not such a shock to the people living in the area, since, as we have seen, English soldiers had garrisoned the town at various periods during the Nine Years War. A charter dated 15 November 1611 was granted to the town by James I. It stated that Cavan town was then the only place of trade and commerce in the county, and where the justices of assize and gaol delivery could conveniently hold sessions. The charter also stated that 400 acres lying in and about the town had been allocated for the maintenance of a corporation to be established there. The charter further stated that 'the said town and place called the Cavan in the said County of Cavan and all that circuit and extent of land lying within the compass of one mile every way around the said town to be measured and taken from the stone house or castle wherein Walter Bradee, gent., now dwelleth, the castle of Cavan, commonly called Reily's castle, and the two poles of land called Rossgolgan excepted, shall from henceforth be called and be the Borough and town of Cavan.'[14]

The boundaries of Cavan town were thus defined and a sovereign, portreeves and council were nominated, among them Hugh Culme, who also held Clogh Oughter castle. The right to hold a market in Cavan town on Tuesdays had been granted to John Binglie in 1603. The charter of 1611 also provided that two annual fairs of two days duration each be held on 14

September and 1 November.[15] Even in the county town, however, there were arguments over the best means of making the plantation a success. Eight poles of land held by the Cavan corporation in the barony of Tullyhaw was the cause of controversy in 1622. It was reported that this land was not being used 'to the best behoof of the town, amongst whom there is much contention, which makes the town not prosper as it should do'.[16] Disagreements of this nature illustrate the various factions and problems which quickly sprang up during the plantation process.

Other settlements grew up outside Cavan town itself. Moynehall was settled by Thomas Moyne, the then Church of Ireland bishop of Kilmore. At Moynehall was built 'one fayer bawne of lyme and stone' within which was a three-story castle containing '26 fayer roomes, with two flankers for the defence thereof'. Along with this, was built a 'towne or village havinge 24 English-like howses and more, all inhabited with Englishe and Britishe families, in performance of the said plantation'.[17]

Killeshandra was another area which was planted during this time, with John Hamilton selling his stake in the town to Frederick Hamilton, who eventually planted the area.[18] The plantation process had not had much success in this area, however. Although there were 20 houses in the town, a substantial number, the inhabitants had been forced to build the houses and plant themselves in the area at their own cost. The town eventually grew, and there were later '34 English-like houses' in Killeshandra, along with markets and fairs for the British of the town. Killeshandra was quite well defended, with a castle nearby and '78 Brittish men of all sorts, with armes, vizt. 24 shot & 54 pikes and half pikes, besides some swords and daggers'. This protection was necessary, however, as most of the area was still occupied by the native Irish, with no other 'town or place within 8 myles distant of the said town of Killeshandra'.[19]

Belturbet was an important social, business and religious centre in the early 17th century. A government proposal that Belturbet should be developed and endowed with land was undertaken in 1609 by Sir Stephen Butler, a native of Bedfordshire, who established a corporate town on 484 acres there the following year.[20] Unlike many of his colleagues, Butler was a conscientious undertaker who, by the autumn of 1611, had planted 41 British families in Belturbet and its hinterland. Butler had leased out most of the land that he had been granted in the area and was building houses there as well as a smith's forge.[21] He had also built a sturdy castle and bawn at Clonosey outside Belturbet, where, for the protection of the area, he kept 'very good Arms'.[22] By contrast, Sir Hugh Wirrall, another landowner in the area, was still living in an 'English thatched house' until the 'accomplishment of his greater work'.[23] A commission in 1611 estimated that Butler could arm 200 men with weapons, even though he was only responsible for 139 adult men at the time.[24] It was reported in 1622 that Butler kept 'but smale store of armes in the Castle, but he [Butler] told us he had dispersed much amongst his tenants and others for their safeguard in the county'.[25] In the face of a threatened insurrection in 1624, however, what little gunpowder there was in Belturbet was no longer held by the settlers, but was in the hands of the native Irish.[26] This gunpowder shortage would worsen as part of Lord Deputy Thomas Wentworth's licensing scheme of the 1630s which only allowed private buyers to purchase small quantities of powder.[27] The arms situation steadily deteriorated and by 1630, Butler only had 30 swords and seven pikes between 164 men. This situation was to have serious repercussions for the settlers in Cavan during the 1641 rising, with one Arthur Culme remarking that at the time of the rising he had in his house 'ten pounds worth of sugar and plums, yet he had not one pound of powder, nor one fixt musquet for the defence of it'.[28]

Not everyone allowed their arms situation to deteriorate to such a degree, however. In 1622, Sir Thomas Waldron in the barony of Loughtee had built a castle and almost completed the construction of a stone house within a bawn. Within the castle were 'very good armes and a drum' as well as 'armes which the chief tenants are bound to keepe'. In all, 71 men, 'very well armed with a leader and a drum before them in a warlike manner', were reported in the barony that year.[29] The general lack of adequately-armed settlers was a common occurrence in settlements across Ulster, however, with Wentworth commenting that the settlers were 'a company of naked [unarmed] men'.[30] As we have seen, such a lack of arms would come back to haunt the settlers by the time of the 1641 rising.

Belturbet received its charter in 1613, and a survey soon after stated that the corporation 'goeth well forward'.[31] In 1619, there were 'houses built of cage-work all inhabited with British tenants, and most of them tradesmen, each of these having a house and garden plot, with four acres of land, and commons for certain numbers of cows and garrons'.[32] By 1622, Butler had built 34 houses in Belturbet, two corn mills and a fulling mill, employing bricklayers, carpenters and smiths to construct them.[33] Yet tensions between the British undertakers and their tenants were evident even at this early stage as the tenants complained that they had not yet been granted the portion of land due to them.[34] The settlers were also unhappy at the number of native Irish still living in Belturbet who were willing to pay higher rents for properties, feeling that they could 'gett no reasonable bargains till the Irish be removed'.[35] Such a situation was advantageous to undertakers such as Butler, as the Irish would pay higher rents than the British settlers. This state of affairs was not to last long, however. In Cavan, large planter estates quickly absorbed the Gaelic freeholds and land in the hands of the native Irish dropped from 20 per cent in 1610 to 16 per cent by 1641.[36] The Breifne region had experienced a period of economic prosperity at the end of the 15th century when the O'Reilly was able to mint his own coin.[37] One hundred years later, however, the region was in ruins following the Nine Years War which had devastated much of Ulster.[38] Throughout the early 17th century, the native Irish across Ulster also had to battle unemployment and struggle with crop failures in financially straightened circumstances.[39] Many of the native Irish now felt that they occupied an inferior social position to the settlers and began to harbour resentment towards the British.[40]

The tensions between the native Irish and British settlers were becoming more apparent during this period. An insurrection scare in the county led by the McGovern clan in 1624 forced panicked British settlers in Belturbet to flee to nearby towns to obtain gunpowder with which to defend themselves.[41] This, and later unrest in 1627, may have been the result of the starving hordes of both native Irish and settlers reported in Cavan in 1629.[42] Yet, there is also evidence of community interaction in planted areas. A number of native Irishmen, including one Donnell Bacach McShane O'Reilly, were involved in land transactions with Butler in 1614.[43] As we shall see, a native Irishman with this name saved an English settler from death in 1642. It is possible, if it is indeed the same person, that O'Reilly's early business trans-actions with Butler had strengthened his relations with sections of the settler community. Lieutenant Arnold Cosby, a British settler in Cavan, possessed an Irish harp before the 1641 rising, indicating his interest in aspects of Gaelic Irish culture.[44] In Leitrim, settler families sent their infants to live with native Irish wet-nurses. Although there is no known evidence of this in Cavan, marriages had begun to take place between the settler and native Irish communities in the 1630s. Richard Parsons, for example, a Protestant cleric based in Drung, was married to an Irishwoman.[45] Nevertheless, unlike Cavan town, whose corporation included representatives of the Old English and native Irish, Belturbet's corporation, despite the prevalence of native Irish in the town, was made up exclusively of settlers and deemed to be very English in character.[46]

Stephen Butler set land aside towards the provision of a Protestant church for the settlers in Belturbet, but it was reported in 1622 that although the town had a Protestant minister residing in the area, there was still 'a great store of Protestants in and about the towne and there should be a church builded there'.[47] By the 1630s, a church, along with native Irish clergy had finally been provided for the town's Church of Ireland Protestant population and Belturbet had become the largest town in the county. William Bedell remarked that Belturbet was the 'only considerable town in the whole county' and that Cavan town itself 'was not so big by one half as Belterbert'.[48] Indeed, 35 of the 1641 deponents in Cavan gave Belturbet as their address, more than any of the other sizeable towns in the county, such as Cavan or Virginia.[49]

Part of the reason for the town's economic success was its location. Belturbet had been chosen as a suitable area for plantation because it was felt to be 'a fitt place to be strengthened with a ward or other residence of civill people and well affected subiectes by reason it lies vpon the head of Loughern'.[50] Situated by the River Erne, then known as the Blackwater,[51] Belturbet was the centre of a thriving waterways industry in the early 17th century.[52] Many boats were moored in the town from whence they would transport assorted goods to various markets throughout Ulster. They were built in Belturbet by entrepreneurs who were quick to take advantage of the recent arrival of people into the area.[53] By 1611, Butler and Sir Hugh Wirrall had built five boats in partnership together.[54] Butler also constructed a watermill and employed people to work there as well as on his boats.[55] John Fishe, who lived at a castle in Lisnamaine, Drumlane, had two boats moored at Belturbet, one weighing ten tonnes and the other weighing six tonnes.[56] In 1618, one John Taylor was granted the right to hold markets and fairs in the town.[57] The economy of the town continued to strengthen and by 1641, there were at least five merchants, two carriers, one baker, one clothier, one cobbler, one gunsmith, one feltmaker, one butcher and one innkeeper who also owned a tannery in Belturbet.[58] Indeed, there had been a tavern in the planted town as early as 1613.[59] The town and its hinterland also held some religious significance in the county. The high cross in Belturbet and the nearby abbey at Drumlane were both visible and constant reminders of traditional Catholicism in an area that had recently witnessed a significant influx of Protestants.[60] As one of the most obvious differences between the settler and native communities, the issue of religion and its implementation was to prove a very contentious one in Cavan and its diocese of Kilmore in the 17th century.

2. Religion in Cavan, 1609–41

The Tudor reformation process made very little impact in the diocese of Kilmore in the 16th century. Although certain bishops, such as Edmund Nugent and John Garvey had allied themselves with the Protestant state at various times, through a mixture of corruption, apathy and absenteeism their efforts were met with little success.[1] Additionally, the activities of 'a lewde friar come from Rome' in 1584 had increased the difficulties of those attempting to impose both political and religious reform in the area.[2] Following the death of Richard Brady in 1607, the diocese of Kilmore was not to have a Catholic bishop, nor even a vicar apostolic, until 1625.[3] This meant that clergy were given free reign in the diocese, permitted to do as they pleased, an opportunity it seems that they were keen to exploit. The diocese which Cavan native Hugh O'Reilly entered upon the beginning of his episcopacy in 1626 had fallen upon hard times.[4] Richard Brady, whose health had long been in decline before his death and who had sought to retire from his position, was not a capable administrator, and church organization was in tatters by 1607, mirroring the general malaise in the area at the time.[5] The churches of the diocese, 17 of which were being used for religious ceremonies, were derelict, with some repaired following the plantation and appropriated by the settlers for Protestant services. The Franciscans had been driven from their abbey of St Mary's in Cavan, and were forced to travel in disguise and celebrate Mass in the countryside and private homes.[6] Drumlane abbey had been leased to Aodh O'Reilly, the chief of the O'Reillys, in 1570. The site was leased to Hugh Strawbridge in 1581 who held it until 1586, when it was leased to Sir Lucas Dillon, holder of various positions in the Pale government, whose family held possession of the site until the turbulent 1640s.[7] Clerical abuses were rife, with lax discipline reported by the exasperated bishop of Kilmore. O'Reilly, described in 1646 by a visiting cleric as 'a man of noble birth, great influence, prudence, learning, goodness [and] noble heart', ordered his clergy to buy gold or silver chalices instead of cheap pewter ones. He asked that their vestments be 'clean and becoming' and threatened to deprive any priests engaged in 'improper conversation and illicit acts', which indicates a certain degree of laxness in clerical celibacy in the diocese. He also asked that ecclesiastical houses or neat oratories be erected in every parish.[8] Whether or not his clergy actually carried out their orders, O'Reilly's attempts to reform his diocese along post-Tridentine lines made him no friends in the diocese, either among the clergy or the laity. Annoyed by this unwelcome episcopal interference, these parties accused the bishop in the secular courts of attempting to exercise papal jurisdiction in the diocese, an accusation for which O'Reilly would be imprisoned in 1637 for six months.[9] O'Reilly was also unpopular with the government, who tried to have him arrested for performing his episcopal functions shortly after his appointment as bishop of Kilmore.[10] The British authorities proved unwilling to crack down on Catholic activities during this period for fear of provoking the ire of Catholic Europe, which only served to increase the difficulties which Protestant clerics in the diocese found themselves in.

As it turned out, O'Reilly did not have much time to implement his reforms as he was appointed archbishop of Armagh in 1628. He did, however, continue to live in the diocese with his family, it being standard practice in poorer dioceses at the time for clerics to live with their families as benefices were often too poor to live upon.[11] O'Reilly reported in 1629 that 'to the great benefit, peace and quietness of the country I have frequently adjusted and settled the law suits and quarrels of the nobles, gentry and people', and that 'by using various means I have banished from my territories thefts, robberies, drunkenness and various pests of the state', a claim which is impossible to prove.[12] Nevertheless, George Creighton, the Virginia Church of Ireland minister, claimed that in 1640 some 80 children were 'unlawfully begotten' in his parish, and it has been suggested that Creighton meant that these baptisms had not been recorded by the established church. It is not known whether they were baptised by a Catholic clergyman, but it seems more likely that this was the case. William Bedell also claimed in 1630 that there were twice as many Catholic clergy (66) in the dioceses of Kilmore and Ardagh than Protestant, that Killinkere was entirely Catholic in 1631 and that the Old English were 'almost universally Catholic' and 'the Irish without exception'. This, along with Dean Henry Jones' claims in 1642 that the inhabitants of Cavan town were 'the most part … Irish and papists', indicates that perhaps the proselytizing work of O'Reilly and his successor did not fail entirely. It is also possible that a rumoured friary in Killinkere may have proselytized the local community there.[13] Of course, it is important to remember that there is a vast difference between passive and staunch Catholicism. Writing in 1646, Dino Massari, Cardinal Rinuccini's representative, made mention of a ruined Cistercian monastery on Trinity Island in Lough Oughter. In this monastery, there were 'many painted and gilt images of saints carved in wood', which were 'now lying exposed to wind and rain, having been overturned by the heretics who dominated the district'. Although Massari claims to have 'found the inhabitants well instructed in the doctrines of the holy faith', it is telling that, although the area had been in Catholic hands since late 1641, no Catholics had attempted to pick up the icons until Massari arrived almost five years later.[14]

Following O'Reilly's transfer to the archbishopric of Armagh in 1628, Eugene MacSweeney from Donegal was appointed bishop of Kilmore, although he was not consecrated until early 1630.[15] Despite O'Reilly's claims to have improved the state of the diocese, it is unlikely that MacSweeney's initial appraisal of the diocese was much different from his predecessor. Another reformer from the same mould as O'Reilly, MacSweeney contended the rights of the abbeys of Kells and Fore to hold 22 parsonages in Kilmore between them. Owning the advowsons to these benefices meant that the abbeys had the right to present whomever they wished to serve the benefice, which the bishop of Kilmore was powerless to prevent. It also meant that much of the revenue of an already impoverished diocese was ending up in the hands of the priors of Fore and Kells. Hugh O'Reilly, in a letter from 1630, explained to the Vatican authorities that, although diocesan revenues only amounted to 600 French florins a year, 100 florins of the meagre total still ended up in the hands of the prior of Fore.[16] The outcome of this case is unknown, but indicates the financial difficulties experienced by the Catholic Church in Kilmore.

MacSweeney was not only interested in financial reform, he was also committed to the correction of his clergy, who had resisted similar moves by Hugh O'Reilly. In a letter from the 1630s, MacSweeney related his troubles to Rome, stating that 'I used assemble my clergy and in those assemblies drew up many salutary statutes for the reformation both of clergy and laity', and had made annual visitations. So unpopular were these measures with his clergy, however, that the troubled bishop claimed to have suffered 'various persecutions and molestations, both from certain contumacious clergymen and from laymen'. Like O'Reilly, MacSweeney was frequently cited by his own clergy to appear before secular tribunals, a move which he always resisted, as to do so would damage his ecclesiastical immunity.[17] The bishop did claim, however, that 'I have been compelled not alone to go into hiding but even to withdraw from my diocese', such was the hostility shown towards him by the clergy and laity in Kilmore.[18] The financial insecurity of the diocese along with the difficulty he was receiving from his clergy led MacSweeney to apply for the post as bishop of Derry, a request which was turned down.[19] MacSweeney continued to serve in the diocese of Kilmore and attempted to reform the settler populace and those from the native Irish community who had adopted the Protestant faith. By the mid-1630s, MacSweeney claimed to have converted 'sixty heretics, or thereabouts'. The bishop seems to have taken this aspect of his episcopacy very seriously; in March 1642, following the synod of Kells held by the bishops and vicars of the ecclesiastical province of Armagh, MacSweeney claimed to have converted 3,000 Protestants to Catholicism, an impressive assertion which must be tempered by a report that the bishop was drinking in an alehouse in Virginia when he made this boast. The bishop's well-documented fondness for whiskey and brandy may have increased the figures quoted.[20]

5 Bishop William Bedell

Although some Scottish and English Catholics received land in Cavan during the plantation, most settlers were Protestant, necessitating the construction of churches and clergy to preach in them.[21] Regular visitations were also held, and the report made in 1622 sheds much light upon the established church in Kilmore at the time. The deanery of Kilmore was held by John Hill, BA, who was resident in Togher, in 1622.[22] Both the archdeaconry of Kilmore and the benefice of Annagh[23] were held by William Andrewes, MA, who lived in Belturbet in 1622.[24]

In 1622, there were two Catholic priests who had converted to Protestantism: Hugh McConnye, who had been 'suspended for misdemeanours' and Shane O'Gowan, who resided in Killinkere. Bedell's son may have exaggerated when he stated that there were no Protestants there.[25] Another member of the O'Gowan family, Nicholas, had been educated at Trinity and anglicized his name to Smith. This was the type of attitude it was hoped that more Irish clergy would display, but it was not to be, and many who had become Protestant later returned to the Catholic fold.[26] Among the 20 clergy mentioned in this document, at least 12 were pluralists, holding more than more ecclesiastical benefice. Although this number of Protestant clergy had risen to 32 by William Bedell's episcopacy in the 1630s, many were still pluralists.[27] This made reform very difficult, as they could obviously not be resident in all of their benefices at the one time. Theoretically, pluralists were required to hire a curate to carry out the ecclesiastical duties in the benefice from which the cleric was absent, but the only one we definitely know to have done this was William Andrewes in Annagh.[28]

When Thomas Moyne died in 1629, William Bedell, the provost of Trinity College Dublin, was appointed as Church of Ireland bishop of

Kilmore and Ardagh, being consecrated in Drogheda on 13 September that year.[29] Born in Essex, William Bedell was a gifted linguist and began to learn Irish in 1628 from an Irishman named Muircheartach Ó Cionga (anglicized as Murtagh King), who later helped Bedell to translate the Old Testament into Irish.[30] Bedell was an accommodating man with experience of life in Catholic countries (he spent some time in Venice), and hoped to instigate, through dialogue and persuasion, a sweeping series of reforms in the diocese which would convince the Catholics there to convert willingly to Protestantism.[31] To this end, he printed in 1631 a short catechism both in English and Irish, and distributed it throughout the diocese. Work also began with Murtagh King and James Nangle on translating the Old Testament into Irish, although this work did not see the light of day until 1685.[32] Bedell favoured the preferment of native Irish to livings in Kilmore, such as the one he gave to a friar named Daniel O'Creane. He also ordered his clergy to open schools in which the English language and Protestant doctrine could be taught.[33] Bedell's practice of appointing Irish-speaking clerics to livings in Kilmore may have caused resentment among established Protestant clergy in the diocese. As the bishop explained to them, he could not see how 'they [English-speaking clergy] would be able to do any good unless they had the language of the people'.[34] There had, however, been some attempts to accommodate Irish speakers in the Church of Ireland before Bedell's arrival in the diocese. John Garvey, a native Irish speaker who was formerly archdeacon of Meath and dean of Christ Church cathedral, had been presented to the see of Kilmore in 1585. But Garvey did not reside in the diocese, so never had the means to exercise his ecclesiastical jurisdiction.[35] When he was appointed archbishop of Armagh in 1596, the see was left vacant before being filled by Robert Draper, who does not seem to have made any attempts to accommodate the Irish language. This was the prevalent attitude throughout the early 17th century, and in 1622, only William Andrewes provided £10 a year to an Irish curate in the parish of Annagh to celebrate 'divine service in the Irish tongue'.[36]

Although his initial contact with the local population was not a success, Bedell quickly established an easy rapport with his Catholic neighbours and made friendly overtures to Archbishop Hugh O'Reilly, who lived nearby.[37] What he found in the diocese in 1629 was not to his satisfaction, however. Many of the churches were in ruins, and his own cathedral was 'without Steeple, Bell or Font'. This despite that the cathedral had been reported 'newly built and repaired' in 1622 by Thomas Moyne with the help of £175 from the archbishop of Armagh, which had been raised from recusancy fines. The parish church of Lurgan was ruinous and it was recommended that a new church be built in Virginia itself.[38] In 1622, the church in Annagh was in no fit condition for worship, described in the visitation of that year as being 'ruinous [and] unfit to be repaired'. Moves were being made, however, to provide Belturbet with a new Protestant church, which had been built by the time Bedell entered the diocese in 1629. The church in nearby Kildallan was also ruinous in 1622, and there were only two churches in Leitrim in reasonable repair. Nor was there a house for the cleric in Castletara in 1622, and the church there was ruinous also. Because of the distance between Casteltara and Ballyhaise, it was decided that it would be a better idea to build a new church in Ballyhaise itself for the settler community there.[39]

This was not the only problem encountered by Bedell on his entrance into the diocese. Kilmore was the poorest diocese in the archdiocese of Armagh, a position which would affect the fortunes of those entrusted with bringing about reforms.[40] The wealth of the benefices influenced, to some extent, the success of the reformation in an area. If benefices were wealthy, they usually attracted well-educated and enthusiastic ministers who were capable of introducing meaningful reform. As we shall see, however, this was not normally the case in Ireland, and the poverty of the livings, along with their unwieldy size, reduced the ability of those entrusted with successfully implementing reform to carry out their duties in a meaningful and lasting manner.

It has been estimated that £19 was the minimum amount on which a rector or vicar could live comfortably in Ireland in the early modern period.[41] None of the benefices in Kilmore in 1588 reached that figure, however, with 20 of them not even managing to reach double figures.[42] There was some improvement by 1617–18, however, with two benefices, the vicarage of Annagh and the combined vicarage and rectory of Castletara worth £30 and £20 respectively.[43] In 1634, Belturbet was described as 'a comfortable place for residence' and the rectory was estimated to be worth an annual sum of at least £300.[44] Although the value of benefices was on average twice as much as in the neighbouring diocese of Ardagh, the clergy in Kilmore were still very poor in comparison with other planted dioceses in Ulster.[45]

The difficult financial situation experienced by the Church of Ireland in the early modern period was exacerbated by bishop's alienating church property, or episcopal temporalities, as a means of raising capital and supplementing their income. Episcopal temporalities were parcels of landed properties and dwellings that could be used to generate income for the running of the diocese. Upon their accession, bishops were often forced to spend considerable time and energy attempting to regain episcopal possessions which had been impropriated or alienated by their predecessors to friends and family members, frequently at an attractive price for the buyer. As an important source of revenue for the bishop, however, the alienation of these temporalities was a serious blow to the finances of the diocese, especially since the leasees sometimes failed to pay the bishop what he was owed. According to his biographer, Bedell opposed this practice, and instead attempted to retrieve some of the lands which previous bishops had leased away. Indeed, he even entered into a lawsuit against the widow of Thomas Moyne in his quest to return to the church what had been leased away.[46] This was not a new problem, however. In 1613, John Davies stated that clergymen indulging in this practice were robbing the church, leaving very little left for their successors.[47] Financial difficulties were exacerbated in the diocese as glebelands in Leitrim were for the most part 'laid out in most unprofitable places and remotest from the church', making it difficult for the established church to claw its way out the financial difficulties it was experiencing.[48]

Before the reformation, rectorial tithes had often been appropriated for the upkeep of religious houses, such as those at Drumlane, Cavan, Kells and Fore.[49] This meant that, following their dissolutions, these advowsons were granted to the lay community. It is possible that these patrons would have appointed conformist reading ministers to benefices in their gift at little cost and diverted the remainder of the funds to support recusant priests. Despite monitoring the situation, no positive action ever seems to have been taken by the authorities to prevent it. The problem was permitted to escalate to the point where any attempts to rectify the matter were hopeless. Recusant patrons were a great impediment to reform and the Irish authorities in the late 16th and early 17th centuries must take a large proportion of the blame for failing to address properly the problem in Ireland during the Tudor and early Stuart periods.[50]

The church into which Bedell entered in Kilmore in 1629 experienced all of the same kind of abuses as had been seen throughout Ireland. Pluralism was one such abuse which he was determined to stamp out, so much so that he resigned from the see of Ardagh in 1632 to allow a resident bishop to take it, stating that he 'was loth myne owne example should serve for a pretext to the detestable practice of many of our own nation' and reckoning that others may follow his lead.[51] Bedell instead attempted to rid the diocese of pluralist clergy, or at least provide adequate curates for parishes not served by their own vicars. This problem was occasionally solved by the appointment of a stipendiary curate to assist in the running of the benefice, as William Andrewes did in Annagh in 1622, but Bedell claimed that this was not a regular occurrence in the diocese.[52] Pluralism was sometimes felt to be a financial necessity in the quest to attract educated ministers to Ireland. It was also closely linked to absenteeism, for if an incumbent held several livings, one or more of these livings had no resident minister. Nevertheless, the problem of pluralism and absenteeism was partly the fault of the patron who appointed the ministers to their benefices. The revenue of several of these benefices were so small that they were unable to support an incumbent and his family. It was decided, therefore, that the best solution to this problem was to present the incumbent to a number of these small livings in order to provide him with the necessary means of support. In 1622, commissioners reported that many clergy were forced to serve several cures as the holders of the advowsons only paid them a fraction of what the benefice was actually worth, meaning that pluralism was their only means of raising enough money to support themselves and their families.[53]

Reform was made even more difficult by the unwieldy size of many the parishes and the large population. This problem was exacerbated by the fact that the advowsons were held by different men, many of whom were recusant and unwilling to co-operate with the bishop's plans for providing suitable clergy to the benefices in their control.[54] Of the 35 benefices mentioned in 1622, 16 were held by Thomas Fleming, eight by the earl of Westmeath, three by Lord Dillon and only three by the bishop of Kilmore.[55] As some of these patrons were recusants, it was very difficult for Bedell to exercise his authority in the diocese in a meaningful way. Bedell's difficulties with pluralists and recusant patrons or even Protestant patrons who opposed him can be seen in the problems the hapless bishop experienced with a Scottish cleric named William Bayly. In 1637, Bayly was presented deacon in the diocese by John Greenham, a local landowner whose brother-in-law had been Thomas Moyne. Although Bedell admitted him on the understanding that Bayly only hold the one living, within one month he had secured a dispensation to hold two additional benefices, provided that they were within 30 miles of each other. When questioned by Bedell, Bayly claimed that his first living was not worth enough to feed and clothe him, even though Bedell claimed that its value was £50 per annum. Bayly was then priested outside the diocese by the bishop of Kilfenora, the father in law of Alan Cook, the chancellor of the diocese and an opponent of Bedell's reforms. Bedell finally suspended Bayly when the cleric secured a presentation to the vicarage of Denn, the second living in the presentation of John Greenham. With the help of Cook, Bayly unsuccessfully appealed to the lord deputy, Thomas Wentworth. Bayly then sought, no doubt at the instigation of Cook, to obtain Murtagh King's living in Templeport for himself, citing the lord deputy's right of presentation there, Murtagh's Catholic family and neglect of his cure. Bayly's actions led to King's deprivation, imprisonment and a fine of £100, leading the beleaguered cleric to give up his living, much to annoyance of Bedell who attempted to have Bayly excommunicated. It is possible that King had made himself unpopular in the diocese following his refusal to administer Holy Communion to one man who was in dispute with another, stating that the man 'was not in charity'. Additionally, Greenham would not have liked Bedell, who had brought Moyne's widow to court over the alienation of church property.[56] Although it is not known how the Bayly/King dispute resolved itself, it is interesting to note the tacit support which the church gave to Bayly in his attempt to hold as many livings to himself.[57]

Upon his entry into the diocese, Bedell set about addressing the many grievances which the local community had with the Church of Ireland in Kilmore. The Catholic community regarded the Church of Ireland as an instrument of exploitation who collected tithes and dues for a church not wanted by them. In Ireland, the church courts were not under the jurisdiction of the ecclesiastical authorities. Rather, they were run by secular laymen with an eye for an easy profit, who had little interest in the state of religion in the diocese. These professionals, often suspected of corruption, charged exorbitant fees and forced Catholics to pay huge fines for their recusancy.[58] Writing in 1629, Archbishop James Ussher noted that 'in my late visitation of Ulster I found nothing so generallye complained of, as the uncertaintye of the payments of tithes'.[59] The main practitioner of this abuse in the diocese was Alan Cook, the chancellor, who had been earlier hauled up before the authorities only to be acquitted on a technicality. Bedell believed that of all the impediments to his reform plan, none was 'greater than the abuse of Ecclesiastical Jurisdiction'. He immediately decided to rid the diocese of Cook's influence, using legal technicalities in the attempt to strip Cook of his title. But there were many in the diocese who had a vested interest in maintaining the *status quo*, and Bedell found it difficult to find anyone willing to represent him in court against Cook, whom Bedell claimed the Irish had nicknamed 'Pouke' and feared 'like the fiend of hell'. In the meantime, Bedell suspended Cook and sat in court throughout his diocese hearing causes and attempting to deliver justice to both Protestant and Catholic alike.[60]

His attempts at ecclesiastical reform brought Bedell trouble similar to that which the Catholic bishops of Kilmore experienced. Because of his pronouncements on the invalidity of Cook's patent as chancellor, Bedell was threatened by some of his clergy with a charge of praemunire, and accused of being a Catholic as well as being an Arminian.[61] Bedell's openness to Catholics would have been unpopular in a diocese whose dean, John Hill, had written to Archbishop James Ussher in 1626 begging him to oppose any toleration of Catholicism.[62] Three clerics in Kilmore, George Creighton, Martin Baxter and Robert Whiskins, preached against Bedell, but do not seem to have taken their grievances any further, as Archbishop James Ussher of Armagh had not heard of it. In a letter to Bedell, Ussher dismissed the bishop's attempts at curtailing Cook's activities as akin to 'building Castles in the Air', an attitude which upset Bedell greatly. Ussher advised Bedell against challenging Cook in court over the issue of an invalid patent appointing Cook as chancellor, as Bedell had not the power of a civil magistrate to do so.[63] Losing his case in the civil courts, Bedell was fined £100 by the lord chancellor. The bishop eventually reached a compromise with Cook, who seems to have moderated his views following his success in court, wherein Cook did not pursue his £100, and left church court administration in the hands of the registrar, Richard Ash, an admirer of Bedell's and later an MP for Belturbet.[64] The efforts of William Bedell to alleviate onerous exactions forced upon the Catholic community had caused much controversy, making

the bishop unpopular both among his clergy and much of the lay
population. Religion became an obvious point of contention between the
native and settler communities, causing a deep-seated resentment to grow
between both cultures.

3. The 1641 rising in Cavan

The political climate in England, Scotland and Ireland was rapidly deteriorating in the late 1630s. The king, regarded by many Catholics as their traditional defender, was losing power to a strengthening puritan parliament. This left Catholics in Ireland with little means of voicing their disquiet and unhappiness at Lord Deputy Thomas Wentworth's increasingly oppressive policies there.[1] In late October 1641, spurred on by the deteriorating political situation in the three kingdoms of Ireland, Scotland and England, and influenced by the actions of the Scottish Covenanters, a number of prominent landowners in Ulster resolved to instigate a show of power there to strengthen their negotiating position.[2] The authority of their leader, Phelim O'Neill, never extended beyond Armagh, so his fellow MP, Sir Philip O'Reilly, whose wife was related to O'Neill, took charge of the rising in Cavan.[3] Despite the beliefs of many Protestants, the leaders of this rising were not attempting to overthrow the king and government. Rather, as Philip MacHugh O'Reilly proclaimed in Cavan, the insurgents were attempting to regain lost liberties and address their grievances.[4] Once the rising had begun, however, elements of native Irish society, unhappy with the plantation project and its social and religious consequences also became involved. It was then that the rising began to spiral out of the control of those who had planned it, and instead became an opportunity for those who wished to address their grievances.[5] Protestant settlers came under attack, were often stripped of their clothes and ejected from their homes by the native population. Within a week of the initial show of strength, sensationalist accounts of violence perpetrated against the settlers were on sale to horrified Londoners, who quickly raised over £40,000 in aid for the stricken Protestant settlers in Ireland.[6] Further pamphlets were published, sometimes on a weekly basis, which provided bulletins detailing the latest occurrences in Ireland. For those unable to read, some pamphleteers obligingly included pictures of armed Irishmen attacking naked settlers and forcing them from their property into the harsh winter of 1641.[7]

The initial rising became part of the general civil wars of the three kingdoms which meant that sporadic fighting in Ireland did not cease until 1653.[8] The events of 1641 soon took on mythic proportions, with the relatively few atrocities increasing in number and severity with each telling. Fortunately, many of the incidents during late 1641 and early 1642 were recorded in the aftermath of the violence. Commissions were set

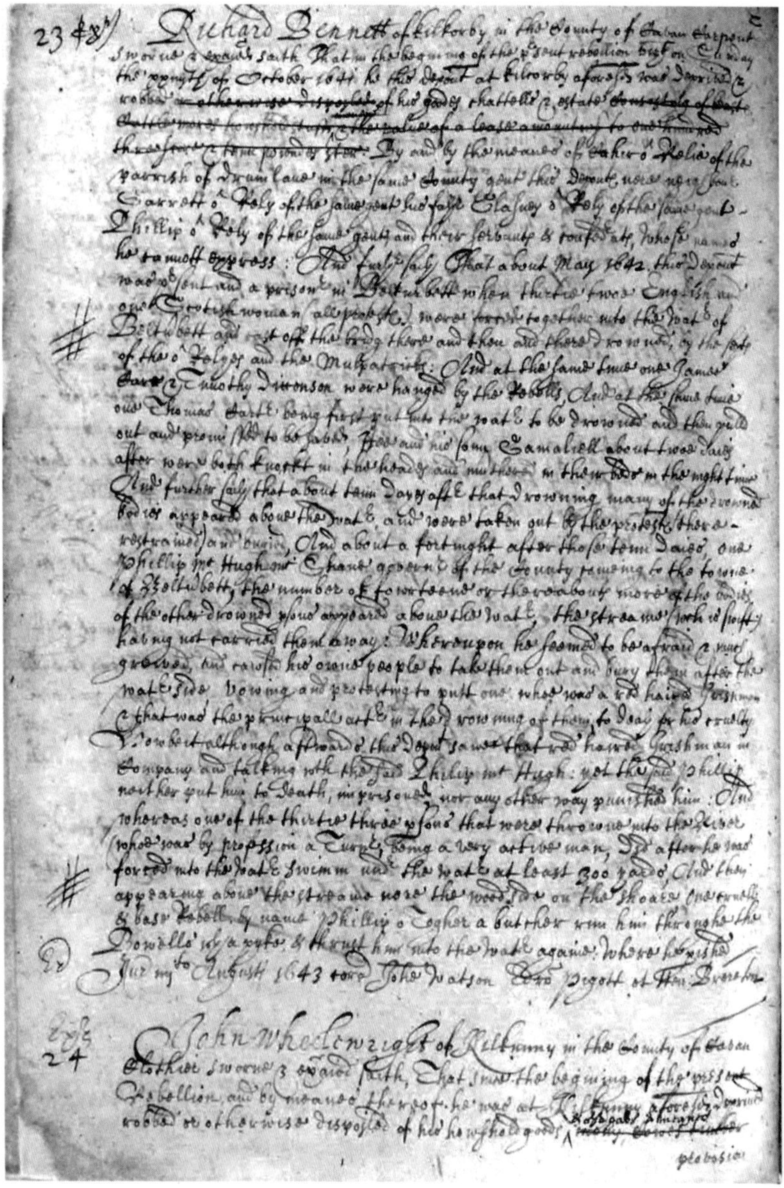

23 (8) Richard Bennett of Kilcorby in the County of Cavan Carpenter sworne & examined saith That in the beginning of the present rebellion viz on Sunday the xxiiith of October 1641 he this deponent at Kilcorby aforesaid was deprived & robbed or otherwise despoiled of his goods chattells & estate By and by the meanes of Cahir o Reily of the parish of Drumlane in the same County gent this deponent's neere neighbour Garrett o Reily of the same gent his sonne Glasney o Reily of the same gent Phillip o Reily of the same gent and their servants & souldiers whose names he cannot expresse: And further saith That about May 1642 this deponent was sent a prisoner in Belturbett when thirtie two English and one Scottish woman all protestants were forced together into the water of Belturbett and cast off the bridge there and then and there drowned, by the said o Reilys and the Musketeers: And at the same time one James Carr & Timothy Dixonson were hanged by the Rebells, And at the same time one Thomas Carr being first put into the water to be drowned and then pulld out and promised to be saved, hee and his sonne Gamaliell about two daies after were both knockt in the head and murthered in their bed in the night time. And further saith that about seaven dayes after that drowning many of the drowned bodies appeared above the water and were taken out by the protestants there restrained and buried, And about a fortnight after those seaven daies one Phillip mc Hugh mc Shane o Reily of the County coming to the towne of Belturbett, the number of fowerteene or thereabouts more of the bodies of the other drowned persons appeared above the water, the streame (which is swift) having not carried them away: whereupon he seemed to be afraid & very grieved, and caused his owne people to take them out and bury them after the waterside vowing and protesting to putt one who was a red haired Irishman (that was the principall actor in the drowning of them) to death for his cruelty Howbeit although afterwards this deponent sawe that red haired Irishman in company and talking with the said Philip mc Hugh: yet the said Phillip neither put him to death, imprisoned nor any other way punished him: And whereas one of the thirtie three persons that were throwne into the River (who was by profession a Surgeon) being a very active man, did after he was forced into the water swimm under the water at least 300 yards, And then appearing above the streame neere the wood side on the shoare one cruell & base Rebell by name Phillip o Togher a butcher runn him through the bowells with a pike & thrust him into the water againe: where he perished

Jur xiiio Augusti 1643 coram John Watson Edw Pigott Hen Brereton

24 John Wheelewright of Kilkenny in the County of Cavan Clothier sworne & examined saith, That since the beginning of the present Rebellion, and by meanes thereof he was at Kilkenny aforesaid deprived robbed or otherwise despoiled of his howshold goods, [illegible] provision

6 Deposition of Richard Bennett

up which collected information supplied by the Protestants in Ireland during the rising regarding attacks, murders, massacres and robberies. Thirty-three volumes of these depositions were collected, which now survive in the library of Trinity College Dublin.[9] Although one historian has estimated that there were only 34,000 British in Ulster at the time of the rising, pamphlets soon exaggerated the official number of British Protestants killed during the rising from the unrealistic 154,000 in 1642 to the incredulous 600,000 in the space of a few short years. By 1754, this number had eventually decreased to 40,000, a still inflated figure which continued to be accepted by some historians into the 20th century.[10] An industry of Protestant historiography concentrating on the grisly detail contained within the depositions sprang up, further stoking anti-Catholic and anti-nationalist feeling throughout Ireland and England for the next 300 years.[11] Even by the 19th and early 20th centuries, accounts of the 1641 rising were coloured by their authors' focus upon notorious and often exaggerated injustices perpetrated against the Protestant population.[12] At the same time, Catholic historians, unsure of what use to make of the contentious depositions, often ignored or derided them. If information from the depositions was used, it was done so with the understanding that the source was unreliable and prejudiced.[13]

Although they have given rise to coloured and emotional accounts of massacres which have been promulgated by anti-Catholic interests, the depositions themselves should not be ignored as valid source material. Only a small number of historians have viewed the depositions in this way in recent times, although this trend is reversing.[14] Beside the nature of anecdotal evidence in the depositions, there is a wealth of incidental detail which can be gleaned from them.[15] While in hindsight a deep-seated resentment seems obvious, the depositions of those interviewed, although occasionally confused and contradictory, contain the only detailed eyewitness accounts of what happened during the rising.[16] The atrocities that did occur were usually exaggerated through hearsay and prejudice. Normally, eyewitnesses to these acts of violence were few in number, and these first-hand accounts are usually the most measured and credible.

The rumour of a general rising reached the settlers in Cavan by 23 October, 1641. Mulmore O'Reilly,[17] the sheriff of Cavan, had collected weapons from Farnham castle outside Cavan town and from other British settlers in the county under the pretence of using them against the insurgents. But it quickly became apparent to the settlers there that O'Reilly was one of the prime movers behind the rising in the county. A faltering attempt at defending Belturbet was made by Sergeant Major Richard Ryves and his small garrison of soldiers. The town had no defensive walls, however, with only the church providing any defensive location, and the people 'resolved to deliver the town to Philip MacHugh O'Reilly, who undertook their protection'. At this, Ryves and his small company of men left Belturbet for Ardbraccan in Co. Meath.[18] The native Irish deposed the old provost and elected one Hugh O'Brady in his place.[19] That evening, the settlers were fired upon and thrown out of their houses. John Parker, then rector of Belturbet, sought sanctuary in Butler's castle at Clonosey, just outside Belturbet.[20] Philip MacMulmore O'Reilly, who was a force of moderation, soon entered the town and announced that any who wished to leave could do so in safety. They would also be permitted to bring some, but not all, of their goods.[21] Protestants who owned cattle were told by O'Reilly that their property would be returned to them once they handed in their weapons.[22] The settlers were also assured that they would have 'free intercourse and liberty of their religion', a promise that was soon broken.[23] Indeed, Philip MacMulmore O'Reilly did intend to keep the settlers and their property in Belturbet safe, but he soon lost control of the situation there.[24] Richard Ash, the town's MP and justice for the peace, who, as we have seen, was previously a supporter of Bedell's, also initially defended the Protestant settlers, demanding the return of their cattle and giving them passes to guarantee their safety as they followed the road to Dublin.[25] His attitude soon changed, however, and he began to threaten truculent Protestants who would not yield their goods with imprisonment. He was later expelled from parliament as a result of his involvement in the rising.[26] The following day, 24 October, Philip returned to Cavan town, but there were no strong fortifications in the town for Captain Bayly to occupy aside from the jail, which was described as 'of no strength to oppose an enemy'. Already lacking sufficient gunpowder, many of Bayly's small force were not in Cavan town at the time and most of those who present were described as Irish 'upon whom he [Bayly] could not rely'. A force estimated at 3,000 entered the town and persuaded Bayly and the settlers there to surrender without recourse to violence, which they did on 27 October.[27] The capitulation of the British settlers in Cavan had been achieved in barely a week.

Over the next week, most of the Protestants in Cavan were forced from their homes and robbed of their goods, so that by 1 November, many of the settlers had been driven out of the towns.[28] John Heron later testified that he found up to 40 armed men outside his house, threatening to knock the door down if he did not open it. Once the insurgents gained admittance, they took all of Heron's goods and drove out everybody from the house. Like many Protestants, Heron and his wife were stripped naked while on the road to Dublin.[29] Before making the final move towards Dublin, many of the settlers dispossessed of their property made their way to various castles and houses kept by Protestant clerics and planters in the county. Frederick Hamilton and James Craig provided such shelter in their castles at Keelagh and Crohan respectively. Although Hamilton had three barrels of gunpowder and provisions for up to six months, the 700 people estimated to have taken refuge with him ensured that these stores were soon empty. It was likewise reckoned that Craig sheltered 120 settlers within his castle.[30] William Bedell also harboured many refugees in his own houses in Kilmore. Although he had no defences at his house, initially 'no violence was used either to his house or his person'. As homeless settlers came to hear of Bedell's charmed existence, they began to descend upon his house in droves, where the bishop 'freely entertein'd all that came, and fill'd all his out-houses with those guests, as many as could sit one by another', despite threats from the native Irish warning Bedell of harm if he continued supporting these refugees. Among those who arrived at his house was the widow of Bedell's predecessor, Thomas Moyne, against whom Bedell had earlier taken legal proceedings for the recovery of episcopal property. Those taking shelter in the bishop's out-houses began to come under attack from the insurgents at night and were forced to leave their sanctuary.[31] Some of the settlers were stripped of their clothes by the Irish and forced to continue towards the capital with nothing to protect them from the harsh winter which Ireland experienced that year.[32] Like so many others, the insurgents stripped Philip Ward from Drumlane of 'his clothes hose and shoes [and] bade him go like a rogue into England'.[33] George Creighton, the vicar of Lurgan, estimated that 1,400 Protestants from Belturbet came through Virginia following the road to Dublin in the hope of finding refuge there.[34]

On the way to Dublin many of the Protestants were attacked by the native Irish and, although helped by people such as George Creighton, a great number succumbed to starvation and exposure before they could reach the capital.[35] It was claimed that many Protestants who had settled in Cavan died at the Hill of Tara while travelling to Dublin.[36] One child of William Atwood's died from starvation and the others had been perilously close to death.[37] Indeed, it was alleged that some of the Protestants were killed by insurgents before they had even left Cavan.[38] Generally, however, it was unusual for these attacks to result in any loss of life.[39] Near Virginia, Nathaniel Clark, while travelling with a group of refugees from Belturbet, was stripped and stabbed in the hand with a pitchfork by an insurgent who threatened to kill him there and then. The insurgents feared that Clark and others like him could return from Dublin armed and ready to carry out reprisals upon those who had attacked them. Threats of this nature occurred quite regularly.[40] One man who did intend to have his revenge upon those who had stripped and robbed him in Belturbet was Thomas Dennibers, who joined the king's army in Dublin soon after arriving there for precisely that purpose.[41]

Although William Bedell had successfully withstood the threats from the native Irish, eventually his luck ran out. As the insurgents became more sure of themselves and their position of power, so too did the frequency of their

7 Clogh Oughter castle

attacks upon the bishop's household increase, both in daring and severity. According to his son Ambrose, the bishop proclaimed that while he 'had a bit for himself never a child there to his power would want'. Edmund O'Reilly then told Bedell 'that he would show him the most woefull spectacle that ever he beheld' and came back the next day with about 200 men on foot and between 20 to 30 men on horseback to force the refugees out, many of whom Ambrose claimed 'perished by the highway with cold and hunger or were killed by the barbarous people'.[42] At one point, Bedell, now almost 70 years old, insisted at gunpoint that the Irish cease their attacks upon settlers on his property, offering himself in their stead. Although shamed into submission at this juncture, the fate of Bedell, finally spurred into direct confrontation with the Irish, was now sealed.[43] From early November until mid-December, Bedell was effectively placed under house-arrest and all of his cattle were taken, but not his corn, which allowed his household to continue to live there. The refugees began to leave Bedell's house and made their way towards Dublin. In early December, James Craig and Frederick Hamilton had taken some as prisoners 'some persons of … quality among the Irish'. This was motivation enough for the Irish on 18 December to eject Bedell from his house, place him under arrest and take his corn for themselves. Eugene MacSweeney was installed in Bedell's house and took over the Protestant cathedral for Catholic worship, with much of Bedell's books and effects destroyed by the insurgents.[44]

Bedell and his party were brought to Clogh Oughter castle, a derelict O'Reilly fortress, and imprisoned there over Christmas 1641, alongside Arthur Culme. The son of Hugh Culme, who had originally planted Virginia, Arthur had been forced to hand over the keys to the castle at the beginning of the rising.[45] Although they were treated quite well, the winter experienced in Ireland that year was unusually severe, which contributed to a break in the elderly bishop's health. Bedell and his entourage were released in early January in exchange for the prisoners taken by Hamilton and Craig. Now that his house had been appropriated by MacSweeney, Bedell himself became a refugee, dependant upon the charity of others. Bedell and his entourage were taken in by a protégé of his, an Irish Protestant cleric named Denis Sheridan, who lived in Drumcorr. However, a fever soon raged through the crowded house, which Bedell finally succumbed to on 7 February 1642.[46] When he died, MacSweeney declared that Bedell should not be buried in Kilmore graveyard, on the grounds that he was a heretic, the standard attitude towards the Protestant dead at this time. So great was the respect which Catholic people had for the Protestant bishop, however, that MacSweeney was over-ruled and Bedell was buried using the Protestant rites with the help of the O'Reillys, who fired a volley of gunshot as his coffin was lowered into the soil, proclaiming '*Requiescat in pace ultimus Anglorum!*'[47] It is not agreed what was meant by this ambiguous salute, which can be translated as 'rest in peace ultimate/best of/last of the English', but it is clear that Bedell was a man admired by all around him, even those who were his titular enemies.

Although most of the Protestant settlers had left Belturbet, some of them were too old or sick to leave with the rest.[48] Others, such as William Gibbs and William Smith, a butcher and smith respectively, were held captive by the insurgents and forced to work for them, a common fate for settlers with trades throughout the province.[49] By about 30 January 1642, the insurgents began to round up a number of British Protestants who were still in the town, much of which had been burned, save for the houses taken over by the native Irish.[50] Two men were stabbed in their beds[51] and Gibbs, together with two other Protestants, Timothy Dickson and James Carr, were carried to the gallows at the outskirts of the town. Both Dickson and Carr were hanged in full view of a number of Protestants, who later examined their bodies. Gibbs was also due to be hanged and the noose was actually around his neck before he was saved through the intercession of one of the insurgents,

Donnell O'Reilly, an acquaintance of his.[52] O'Reilly's intercessions were not enough to save Gibbs' wife from attack, however, and she was beaten so ferociously about the head that she was almost lost an ear and lingered perilously close to death.[53] Donnell O'Reilly then followed the other insurgents to the river where they drowned a number of other remaining Protestants.[54]

There are only two definite eyewitness accounts of the drownings and together they name 36 people who, they claim, were drowned in the river that day.[55] Peter Kirkeber, speaking in 1654, named a number of them, estimating that approximately 37 Protestants had been drowned that day. William Gibbs, speaking in 1643, reckoned that 'about thirty-four British men, women, and children' were drowned at the bridge.[56] The two eyewitness accounts are presented in restrained and factual terms and, as elsewhere in the country, are more credible as a result.[57] Separately, they both name a number of the same people and mention others besides whose names they did not know, usually the children of those known to them.[58] Taking the names supplied in eyewitness accounts into consideration, it is likely that approximately 36 people drowned that day. Other deponents from elsewhere in the county who were not present in Belturbet at the time boosted the numbers killed to 50 and 60, although some estimated it to have been 33 to 35 and even as few as six.[59] It was also claimed by some of these deponents that victims struggling to escape the river were attacked with pikes and shot at.[60] Deponents also reported various murders elsewhere in Cavan as well as in Cos. Monaghan and Fermanagh.[61] These statements, however, were normally the result of speculation and hearsay and the more excessive elements of their depositions should therefore be viewed with some scepticism.

Although mostly made up of Irish people from the immediate vicinity, those responsible for the massacre at Belturbet seem to have been led by insurgents from Leitrim and Fermanagh.[62] Philip MacHugh O'Reilly's wife, Rose O'Neill, who allegedly nurtured a virulent hatred of all British settlers, both Scottish and English, was also at the forefront of the drownings.[63] Massacres of this sort sometimes occurred as a result of Irish military setbacks against the Protestants and it is possible that the insurgents were reacting to the Islandmagee massacre of about thirty Irish by Scottish settlers in January 1642.[64] It also seems that Rose had goaded the insurgents into drowning the Protestants, saying that 'she was never well that day that she saw any of either of those nations [England and Scotland]'.[65] It is important to note, however, that Philip MacHugh O'Reilly himself was not privy to the massacre. Events had spiralled out of his control and he was angered by the incident in Belturbet as the large loss of life had not been part of the original plan devised by Phelim O'Neill. O'Reilly ordered that the bodies of those who had perished be taken from the river and buried, a task which the remaining Protestants had begun to carry out.[66] Although he criticized those responsible, he refused to punish them and continued to be seen in their company.[67] It would, how-ever, be a mistake to believe that this outrage was accepted meekly by all of the Protestants still in the area.

By early 1642, Sir James Craig and Sir Frederick Hamilton had garrisoned their castles at Keelagh and Croghan with 100 and 250 fighting men respec-tively; indeed, their men had been among the best armed in the county in 1630.[68] Hamilton also had 36 horses ready for use against the insurgents. Following the massacre at Belturbet, Hamilton and Craig, who had already burnt Killeshandra to prevent the Irish from using it, were left 'resolved on revenge, they going forth in severall parties, killing and hanging prisoners … thus were all of the rebels used who after their time fell within their power'. Indeed, Hamilton soon acquired a fearsome reputation for cruelty towards Irish prisoners captured by him.[69] In an indication of the thorn which Craig was in the side of the Irish, one insurgent named Nugent was heard plotting how he could ambush James Craig if he could disguise himself and his men with blue bonnets to fool Craig into believing that the insurgents were Scots coming to aid them.[70] A reversal of fortune by June 1642, however, saw the castle held by James Craig full of sickness and famine. Their stores of food had run out, and a siege begun by the Irish meant that there was no way for the settlers within the castle walls to acquire supplies. Indeed, 1,000 men from a force of 1,700 from Cavan who had held been holding siege at Drogheda had been withdrawn in order to reinforce the siege at Killeshandra. Within a few weeks, an estimated 180 settlers had died, among them Craig and his wife. Following James Craig's burial in the church of Killeshandra, his corpse was allegedly disinterred by the Irish and mutilated.[71] Faced with imminent demise, those remaining were forced to surrender to the Irish. On 15 June 1642, roughly 1,200 men, women and children left Cavan for Dublin, so hungry that they were forced to eat the cow hides that had covered the cabins and huts which they had built since the rising began.[72] The first phase of the 1641 rising in the county had reached its end.

So, why did people involve themselves in this bloody and destructive series of events? The lack of evidence relating to the motivations of the native Irish makes it difficult to ascertain their reasons. The only contem-porary accounts we have of their reasons are given to us via the depositions of those who were attacked which can be prejudiced. There are, however, a number of common themes which run through the deponent's claims. On 4 November 1641, Phelim O'Neill published what he claimed was a com-mission from King Charles I authorizing arms to be taken up in his defence in Ireland.[73] Although a forgery, the commission was widely believed to be genuine at the time and many in the native Irish community, such as Philip MacMulmore O'Reilly, took it seriously.[74] Accordingly, Philip MacHugh O'Reilly proclaimed in a speech supposedly written by William Bedell, that the Irish and Old English had been threatened 'either with captivity of our consciences, or losing of our lawful liberties, or utter expulsion from our native seats'.[75] The rising, O'Reilly claimed, was in support of the king, the defender of Catholicism, against Puritan forces in Ireland and England, and Bedell was arrested by Edmund O'Reilly in the name of the king.[76] One group of insurgents claimed that 'they had good reason to do what they did for the Protestants in London had taken the queen, and were minded to put her to death, had killed some of the friars that belonged to her and also had taken the prince to make him king but he refused and he was gone they know not whither'.[77]

When asked by the settlers the reason for their actions, many of the insurgents replied that they had the 'kinges broad seale' for what they had done, a reference to O'Neill's commission.[78] Some took it further, however, claiming that Philip MacHugh O'Reilly was now king and that they would have no more to do with Charles or his family.[79] Another deponent claimed that Philip MacHugh O'Reilly had proclaimed himself lord governor of Ireland.[80] One Owen Reilly, drunk on his new-found power, declared that he and his fellow insurgents 'would not have the king of England to rule over them any more for they had too much of them already but they would be kings themselves'.[81] One deponent testified that he heard some insurgents 'wishing that they had the king of England among them that they might be revenged upon him for sending soldiers against them', even though they had previously claimed to be his soldiers. These insurgents then claimed to be the queen's soldiers.[82]

Elizabeth Poke had been told that some of the insurgents had gone into the church in Belturbet and 'thrust their pikes into and through the king's arms and then pull[ed] them down and trod them under their foot saying they would do as much to his majesty of England if he were in that place'.[83] When given a pass in his majesty's name to enjoy safe passage to Dublin, one deponent was unsure whether the insurgents 'meant his majesty of England or a king of their own making'.[84] Proclaiming a market in the town of Cavan, another insurgent had prayed 'God keep Colonel Rely and not according to the old form of God save the king'.[85] While claiming that they were carrying out the king's wishes, many insurgents often expressed in the same breath their wish to be free of English government and influence, implying their use of the commission as a smokescreen to gain their true anti-plantation objectives.[86]

Religion was another source of contention between the settlers and the native Irish.[87] Although Protestants had initially been assured of their religious freedom,[88] this soon changed as the rising progressed. Fears were rife among the Catholic community that what religious rights they had, which were implicitly recognized by Charles I, were going to be taken away from them.[89] One Irish priest claimed that a statute had been passed in England, forcing all Catholics either to attend Protestant services or face banishment.[90] Others said the king 'was more a papist than a Protestant' and that the Irish had pre-empted the anticipated massacre of Catholics in England.[91] Irish insurgents claimed that 'the English thought to cut the throats of the Irish for their religion but the Irish would prevent them, and cut their throats first for their religion'.[92] The Catholics burned the Bible and Protestant literature at the high cross in Belturbet and elsewhere throughout the county.[93] They insulted the Protestants, denying their status as Christians and instead deemed the settlers to be heretics.[94] Many Irish also refused to bury Protestants in graveyards, despite the fact that Catholics and Protestants often shared the same graveyards at this time.[95] When the insurgents came across a Protestant ceremony, they said that those attending were at 'the Devil's service and it were a good deed to burn the roof over their heads'.[96] In Belturbet on Easter Sunday, 1642, it was alleged that the native Irish fired upon what few Protestants were left in the town as they left their church service.[97] It was also rumoured among the settlers that any Protestant who did not go to Mass by Easter would be hanged.[98] When the Protestants suffered a military setback near Drogheda in November 1642, the Catholics jeered at them in Cavan, saying, 'You English Protestants where now is your god. Now you see that your religion is nought for your god has forsaken you.'[99] In Belturbet, two insurgents dipped copies of the Bible in dirty water and slapped Thomas Taylor and other local Protestants on the face with them, saying, 'I know you love a good lesson here is a most excellent one for you and come tomorrow and you shall have as good a sermon as this.'[1]

As the religious leaders of their areas, the clergy played a prominent role in the uprising. By 1636, there were 28 Catholic parish priests and a number of Franciscan regulars in the diocese of Kilmore.[2] The clergy were seen by Protestants as having a negative influence upon the Catholic populace, with reports made of clergy in league with the insurgents, including one 'rebellious monk' who was 'much given to drunkenness', and Bishop MacSweeney, who was reported in Leitrim as being a 'carrier of arms'.[3] But in actual fact, the religious were normally quite moderate and as the rising spiralled out of control, its supposed leaders appealed to the clergy for help.[4] Clerics attempted to re-direct Catholic ire towards Protestant symbols and objects, rather than the people themselves.[5] A number of deponents reported both priests and laity, particularly a monk, Redmond Fitzsimons, who insisted on giving Protestants the chance to attend Mass and convert to Catholicism, telling them that this was the only way that they could hold onto their goods, an offer which many, but not all, Protestants claimed to have rejected.[6] The alternative was usually prison and/or assault, such as in the case of John Anderson and Arthur Culme, who were imprisoned for their refusal to recant their religious beliefs.[7] Thomas

Grant testified that soon after the rising began, however, a Protestant minister named Parsons 'recanted his Protestant profession and there did swear to continue in the Romish Catholic religion'.[8] As already mentioned, Eugene MacSweeney himself claimed to have converted 3,000 settlers to the Catholic faith.[9] The evangelizing efforts of William Bedell during the 1630s had borne some fruit, evinced by the small number of native Irish who became Protestants during his episcopacy. The rancour displayed by many towards Protestants during the 1641 rising, however, was enough to persuade many Irish to recant their new Protestant beliefs and revert back to Catholicism.

Perhaps the most important factor in the insurgents' participation in the rising was their dislike of the English settlers and jealousy of their relative economic prosperity. One Irishwoman in Belturbet proclaimed that 'I would to God that the skeane [dagger] in my hand were in the hearts of all the noblemen in England'.[10] There were many more anti-English and anti-planter sentiments expressed during this period, and sometimes no distinction was made between the Old English and the new settlers.[11] One group of insurgents, for example, claimed that 'it was time for them to look for their own lands that the English had kept from them for 33 years' and many others expressed similar sentiments that the English should be expelled from Ireland.[12] In Kilkenny in 1648, Mulmore O'Reilly, one of the leaders of the rising in Cavan, sought a review of the plantation process in the hope of recovering lost property.[13] Such specific references to remembered losses that derived from the Ulster plantation were rare, however. Through the seizure of the settlers' property and the destruction of any evidence of debts owed to the Protestant settlers, most of the native Irish were displaying an interest in addressing their more immediate economic problems.[14] According to deponents, a huge amount of goods, chattels and property were lost as a result of the rising, with the native Irish taking their opportunity to settle old scores and cancel debts.[15] The double forge and furnace for iron-smelting at Doobally in west Cavan owned by Charles Coote was ransacked of valuables by the O'Rourkes and others during the rising.[16] Edward Philpott, who had married Stephen Butler's widow, estimated that he and his step-children had lost property worth up to £2,500 and was fearful that he would lose £1,000 annually should the rising continue.[17] John Heron estimated that he had lost lands worth £200 and goods worth £414,[18] while Edmund Sherwin was robbed of goods and chattels worth £150 as well as his horse and sword by Irish insurgents wielding bats and clubs. Some of Sherwin's tenants were also threatened with death if they refused to divulge the whereabouts of a 'great bowle' which their landlord used to drink from.[19] A clothier in Belturbet believed that he had lost annual profits of £20 as a result of the rebellion.[20] More settlers in the county claimed to have lost amounts ranging from £100 to almost £600.[21] They were not to recoup these losses and the Irish burned most of the settler's houses which were not kept for their own use.[22] It is important to note, however, that some of these deponents hoped to receive compensation so may have exaggerated the extent of their losses.[23]

The clergy also seized the moment to improve their financial situation as well as the status of the Catholic Church in Cavan. When William Bedell was imprisoned in the castle at Clogh Oughter in December 1641, the Catholic bishop of Kilmore, Eugene MacSweeney, took the opportunity to take up residence in Bedell's house at Kilmore. He also claimed the Protestant church in Kilmore for the Catholic faith, set up a new altar at it and began to perform Catholic ceremonies there. A Protestant church in Laragh was also re-consecrated by Catholic clergy and used to celebrate Mass.[24] Another priest, known only as Mackbride, broke all of the seats in a Protestant church in Cavan and brought them home to his own house.[25] The Franciscans in Cavan town, who had been living in local private houses during the 1630s, also took the opportunity to reclaim their monastery, and continued to live there for another ten years.[26] It has been suggested that the economic hardships experienced by Ulster clergy may go some way to explaining why clergy were often at the forefront of the disturbances in 1641.[27] Not everyone sought to improve their economic position during the rising, however, and people such as Philip MacHugh O'Reilly and Patrick Plunkett, and Lord Dunsany, were actively involved in assisting the despoiled settler population in Cavan.[28] It is significant that both of these men were relatively wealthy and felt no need to rob the settlers as others had.

In December 1641, Philip MacHugh O'Reilly ordered that the Irish were 'not to meddle with any of the Scottish nation except they give you cause'.[29] Although usually Protestant, Scottish settlers such as George Creighton were usually safe from the insurgents, implying that religion was not the primary motivating factor for some of those involved in the rising.[30] Although as Creighton wondered, 'if religion was the pretended cause of the mischief why would they spare the Scots'?, it was claimed elsewhere that the Irish hatred was 'greater against the English nation than their religion'.[31] Indeed, English settlers seeking refuge with Scots based in Fermanagh often found themselves delivered into the hands of the Irish insurgents.[32] Again, however, some Irish ignored O'Reilly's request and displayed an equal hostility towards the Scots as they showed towards the English, saying that they would be rid of both the English and the Scottish.[33] Two Protestant ministers believed that the Irish were merely pretending to be friends with the Scots in order to pick off the English and Scottish separately, one quoting the Machiavellian proverb 'divide and rule' to that effect.[34] Indeed, some of those drowned at Belturbet were believed to be from Scotland.[35] Arthur Culme later reported that 16 Scottish men had been murdered near Lough Oughter.[36]

Inevitable links had been forged between the native and settler communities, and it seems that these bonds went some way to protecting some settlers from at least immediate attack when the rising began. George Butterwick from Drumlane was confronted by a band of native Irish insurgents who threatened his wife with violence unless she disclosed the whereabouts of rent money which they believed to be hidden in the settler's house. The Butterwicks were only saved when their native Irish servant intervened with the insurgents, convincing them to leave empty-handed.[37] A parish priest staying with the Reynolds family of Lissanore managed to protect the settlers from a band of insurgents who threatened their lives. He also later hid the men of the family from the murderous intent of the insurgents. The fact that he was staying with the family and that he continued to help them as the rising grew in strength and animosity indicates a warm relationship between both parties, a bond that failed to break under the enormous pressure of the rising.[38] As we have already seen, Donall O'Reilly saved William Gibbs, an acquaintance of his, from hanging in Belturbet in January 1642. Yet O'Reilly could ignore the pleas of mercy made upon her knees by one Widow Munday and force her into the river to her death – which indicates that these personal ties did not apply to everyone.[39]

Ties of kinship also saved some of the settlers from possible harm. Richard Parsons, a minister based in Drung, was told that he and his wife, who was related to Philip MacHugh O'Reilly, would have been killed 'but for her kindred's sake'.[40] George Creighton, the Virginia-based cleric, was afforded protection from Philip MacHugh O'Reilly's mother when he convinced her of their kinship 'by the house of Arguile, of which house it seems she was well pleased, that she was descended'.[41] When Philip MacHugh O'Reilly announced their ties of kinship, Creighton believed that this 'bound the hands of the ruder sort from shedding his blood'.[42] Denis Sheridan was another cleric who was allowed to shelter settler refugees at his house and was not harmed, despite his refusal to recant his Protestantism, and his marriage to an Englishwoman.[43] Although Sheridan was Irish, he had been reared from childhood by John Hill, the dean of Kilmore, and Bedell, who liked him and admired his fluency in Irish, promoted him to a living in Killesher, Co. Fermanagh. Despite this, Sheridan's membership of a powerful Irish family in Cavan was enough to protect him from those who would otherwise have done him harm.[44]

So, what was the aftermath of the atrocities committed throughout Cavan? Those who were assaulted often knew their attackers and could name them. The highly personalized nature of these attacks made it impossible for most of them to ever consider a return to the county, particularly as it remained in Irish hands until it fell to Cromwellian forces in 1653.[45] The rising had a huge effect upon those who had witnessed and suffered during it. What had occurred in Ireland during the 1641 rising was unprecedented, and people had difficulty explaining not only the events, but also their reaction to them and their feelings. Much of this uncertainty caused a spiritual crisis in the country that manifested itself in the aftermath of the rising, when people were able to put into words their feelings about what had occurred. In what seems to have been an increasing trend across Ulster, apparitions began to appear in Belturbet following the massacre there, supposedly the ghosts of those who had died in the river.[46] Again, none of those who reported these ghostly apparitions actually saw them for themselves. One man claimed that the apparitions began to appear to Philip MacHugh O'Reilly, leading Philip to have their bodies retrieved from the river and buried.[47] Others described the 'strange visions and apparitions commonly seen on the waters of Belturbet, [which] doth make roarings like as of a bull, strange lights, clapping, [and] singing of psalms', and testified about the 'apparition of a man has been constantly seen, as seeming to stand bolt upright'.[48] Another deponent claimed that although the bodies lay in the water for a long time, they 'were not torn or eaten with fish nor devoured but their skins remained whole'.[49] It was alleged by deponents that these ghostly cries and sightings so scared the Irish soldiers that they deserted their posts, refusing to linger near the scene of the massacre.[50] Following these apparitions, it was alleged that it was impossible to catch any fish up to half a mile away from the spot of the drownings.[51]

This was not the only instance of people attributing supernatural causes to events at this time. William Bedell's biographers spoke of the mysterious death of Lord Deputy Christopher Wandesford, who died suddenly after he had torn a page out of the parliament book. They also mentioned a 'strange multitude of ratts' invading houses, which an old Irishwoman proclaimed were 'a signe of war'. Strange large insects or worms appeared in a field beside Edmund O'Reilly's house, becoming something of a local attraction and ate all vegetation there. It was also reported that a 'mad man', usually a good humoured person, had become very melancholic, asking, 'Where is king Charles now?' and writing that 'We doubt not of France and Spain in this action.'[52] This second statement was held in great significance as it was believed that continental Europe was behind the rising.[53]

All of these signs which may not have attracted much attention in the usual course of events were now held to be of great significance in identifying the origins of the rising. Both sides, however, claimed that God was on their side and had stories to illustrate this. A later report of the escape from Cavan of Faithful Teate, a Church of Ireland minister in Ballyhaise, recounted how his infant child would have died had angels not placed a bottle of buttermilk under the rock which the child and its mother were lying under. This story gained some fame and was repeated and printed many times as proof of God's favour towards the Protestant settlers.[54] George Creighton also attributed his decision to buy a house and unusually large amount of provisions mere weeks before the rising, which he later used to shelter and feed refugees, to God's providence.[55] These examples indicate the massive physical and emotional upheaval experienced by the settlers and their attempts to rationalize it in their own fashion into something which they could understand.[56]

The 1641 rising had a huge and traumatic effect both upon the Catholic and Protestant communities in Ireland at the time. Following this outbreak of violence, the English no longer trusted the Irish Catholics, and by the end of the decade, Oliver Cromwell arrived in Ireland to put down once and for all the rebellious Irish, which he did with ruthlessness. Likewise, the native Irish and the Old English communities formed an uneasy alliance between them in an attempt to gain religious, social and political concessions for themselves. The result was ten years of instability and sporadic fighting, with losses and gains on both sides.

Conclusion

Ten years of intermittent fighting in Ireland followed the violence and upheaval of late 1641 and early 1642. Espying an opportunity to reclaim his family's lost lands, Owen Roe O'Neill, a colonel in the Spanish army, returned from the continent on 8 July to take leadership of the faltering Ulster army, which had been on the verge of surrender.[1] O'Neill set up his camp in Cavan and from now on would regularly use the county as a training ground and base for his armies. Cavan's position as a marcher area on the edge of the Pale, access to the eastern ports, Cavan and Belturbet's roles as provincial meeting areas, the pre-existing fortifications and O'Neill's ties with the O'Reillys (his mother was a daughter of Aodh Conallach O'Reilly) were all factors in the general's decision to utilize the county thus.[2] Following his army's calamitous defeat in Clones on 13 June 1643, O'Neill, by temperament and training a cautious military commander, regrouped his men in Cavan, where he transformed the shambling force into a disciplined army.[3]

Following O'Neill's victory over Robert Monroe, commander-in-chief of the British forces in Ulster, at the battle of Benburb in Tyrone on 5 June 1646, Clogh Oughter castle was used to house a number of officers captured by O'Neill's men.[4] Although King Charles requested that Viscount Montgomery, one of the captives, be released, O'Neill declined, and continued to hold him.[5] Monsignor Dionisius Massari, a representative of the papal nuncio, Archbishop Rinuccini, who had been sent to Ulster to give O'Neill money to continue his campaign, met Montgomery at the castle that same year, along with other colonels and generals held there. Despite their captivity, Massari was still able to make them a gift of 'sheep, young pigs, chickens, cheese, bread, wine, beer and whiskey'.[6] Massari also took the opportunity to visit Trinity Island on Lough Oughter, and there found in the ruined monastery overturned statues of Mary and Child, Mary Magdalen, SS Patrick 'and three other saints'.[7]

Massari was later brought to a fair near Cavan town, where he was amazed by the large crowds and stock available for sale there. Although money was scarce in the county, food was plentiful, and animals and food were sold 'at an absurdly low price'. This seems odd in a county which was at the centre of a war raging all around them.[8] It may have been due to the fact that O'Neill's men went home for the summer to gather in their harvests, leaving their commander unable to fully capitalize on his victory at

45

Benburb.[9] In 1647, O'Neill continued to make military excursions from his base on Gallmagh Hill at Lough Sheelin in Cavan, and set up a new headquarters at Lisnamaine near Belturbet in late 1648.[10]

Following a foray into Derry in 1649, O'Neill's health rapidly deteriorated, and by August of that year, had begun to move southwards with his army. By the time they reached Ballyhaise, O'Neill was so weak, supposedly as a result of tetanus, that he was carried on a horse litter to Clogh Oughter, where he probably resided in Arthur Culme's house on the shore. In one of his last letters, dated 1 November 1649, O'Neill wrote that he was 'on my death bed, without any great hope of my recovery'. Sure enough, five days later on 6 November, O'Neill died, surrounded by such notable Cavan personages as Philip MacHugh O'Reilly, Archbishop Hugh O'Reilly and Bishop Eugene MacSweeney, and was reputedly buried in the Franciscan friary in Cavan town.[11]

Due to its strategic location between the borders of Cavan, Monaghan and Fermanagh, an election was held in Belturbet in March 1650 to elect O'Neill's successor. This fell to Heber MacMahon, bishop of Clogher, whose inexperience in combat soon led to a series of military defeats, the Ulster army being decimated by Charles Coote in Donegal in mid-1650.[12] From this time on, Cromwell's retaking of the province was inevitable, it being only a matter of time before the Ulster army collapsed. The scene of the Ulster army's final days and eventual defeat was played out at Clogh Oughter. Archbishop O'Reilly held a council of the bishops of the province of Armagh at the priory on Trinity Island at Lough Oughter on 29 July 1651. The synod sought to counteract the rise of Protestantism in the area through the reform of church administration and organisation. This was to be O'Reilly's last official act as primate of Ireland, and he died at Trinity Island on 9 January 1652.[13] O'Reilly's last years had seen a reversal in his fortunes so that the state of Catholicism was much the same as when he had briefly reigned as bishop there in 1626. Now he was forced to celebrate Mass in a covert manner and administer confirmation in the woods and hills due to the presence of parliamentary forces in the county. Following his death, O'Reilly was also buried at the Franciscan abbey in Cavan.[14]

By 1653, Cromwellian forces had re-conquered most of Ireland, with only small pockets of resistance remaining around Cavan and Fermanagh. Philip MacHugh O'Reilly, the leader of the severely depleted Ulster army, continued to hold out at Clogh Oughter. By March of 1653, however, parliamentary forces had taken two islands on the lake, including Trinity Island, and were laying siege to the island fortress of Clogh Oughter. The garrison surrendered to Colonel Theophilus Jones on 27 April 1653, whose gunpowder destroyed the castle, leaving the shell that remains to this day.[15]

Even more so than Archbishop O'Reilly, Bishop Eugene MacSweeney experienced many difficulties in the autumn of his life. Although he had been able to carry out visitations throughout the diocese in the early 1640s, when Catholics had once more held possession of the churches, Cromwellian incursions into Cavan soon made this practice impossible. Old, infirm and nursing an alcohol dependency, MacSweeney was initially forced to live in exile in Rossinver, a mountainous area of Leitrim. So total was Cromwellian control in Ireland that from 1654 until 1659 and again from 1661 until 1662, MacSweeney was the only Catholic bishop in the country, permitted to stay only because of his ill-health, being confined to bed from about 1653. By 1657, MacSweeney was referred to as being 'old, decrepit, and bedridden', and was living on the slopes of Sliabh an Iarainn in Leitrim, where he lived out the remaining years of his life like an anchorite. His decline was slow and inexorable, and in 1665, he was again described as bedridden and subsisting on whiskey and brandy. Due to his weakened state, MacSweeney did not conduct diocesan visitations, nor would he nominate a vicar-general and stubbornly refused to accept one nominated by another. Such was the deterioration in MacSweeney's physical and mental health, however, that by 1666, Thomas Fitzsimons was appointed as vicar-general of Kilmore, much to the bishop's displeasure, who resisted his nomination. Fitzsimons' unpopular attempts to install order in a diocese whose clergy revelled in their freedom eventually led to his dismissal and excommunication at a provincial council held near Bawnboy in 1669.

As the primate had died, MacSweeney, in his role as vice-primate, convened this council, probably at the instigation of corrupt clergy under threat of losing their livings, as a means of ridding themselves of the troublesome vicar-general. Thus MacSweeney, a man who had once been subjected to intimidation from his clergy in his attempts to reform them, was now allowing others to torment a similar would-be reformer in his name. In 1669, Fitzsimons was replaced by Robert Plunkett, who only arrived in the diocese following MacSweeney's death on 18 October of that year. The vacant bishopric was not to be filled until 1728. The modest progress made by the Catholic Church during the early days of MacSweeney's episcopacy had been eroded away by the end of his life. The parish system had broken down and the counter-reformation had failed to make any lasting impact in the diocese at this time.[16]

Following the destruction wreaked upon the county during the Nine Years War, a period of stability and rebuilding took place in Cavan. The town of Cavan was rebuilt, settlements such as Belturbet and Virginia were established as part of the plantation process, and it was felt by officials in 1606 that the people of Cavan were open to religious conversion.[17] Clerics such as William Bedell, Hugh O'Reilly and, for a time, Eugene

MacSweeney, attempted to impose reform upon recalcitrant and corrupt clergy, both Protestant and Catholic, and relieve the local population of onerous charges imposed upon them by the ecclesiastical courts. This optimistic approach proved to be a false dawn of hope, however. Any advances made in the county were wiped out by the catastrophic 1641 rising. Many settlers were attacked and deprived of their goods, some were murdered, most shamefully during the massacre in Belturbet. Bishop William Bedell, who had done so much to alleviate the privations suffered by the people of Cavan, both before and after 1641, died as a result of his ill-treatment during the rising. As the centre of operations for Owen Roe O'Neill during the 1640s, Cavan was obliged to support an army, a task which it carried out reasonably well. Much of the county was in ruins, however, and Clogh Oughter castle suffered massive structural damage during Jones' final assault upon it in 1653.[18] The monastery on Trinity Island located on Lough Oughter was also in a state of disarray as a result of the disturbances during the turbulent 1640s. Following a thirty year period of relative peace after the Nine Years War, the county descended back into a state of destruction and turmoil, leaving Cavan in much the same sorry condition as the settlers had found it upon their arrival there. Depleted of any resisting forces, the county, was ready once more for yet another, ultimately more successful, plantation campaign.

Appendices

APPENDIX 1: THE NAMES OF THOSE WHO DROWNED AT BELTURBET
GIVEN IN THE DEPOSITION OF PETER KIRKEBER IN 1654

Timothy Dickson's wife and his two children
Gamaliel Carter's wife and one of his children
The Widow Phillips
Edward Martin's wife and two of his children
John Jones and two of his children
Samuel the hookmaker
The Widow Munday
The Widow Stanton
And several other Protestants to the number of 37 or thereabouts.

Source: Hickson, *Ireland in the seventeenth century*, ii, 303–4.

APPENDIX 2: THE NAMES OF THOSE WHO DROWNED AT BELTURBET
GIVEN IN THE DEPOSITION OF WILLIAM GIBBS IN 1643

John Jones
Cham Carter
Samuel Walsh
William Carter
James Carr's wife
Mrs Phillips
The Widow Mundy
Anne Cutler
Elizabeth Stanton and two of her children and four of her daughter's
    children
Timothy Dickson's wife and four children
William Carter's wife and two of her daughters and two of her
    grandchildren
The rest he cannot tell by name.

Source: deposition of William Gibbs (TCD, MS 832, f.140).

Notes

Anal. Hib.	*Analecta Hibernica.*
Archiv. Hib.	*Archivium Hibernicum.*
Bodl. MS Rawl.	Rawlinson manuscript, Bodleian library, Oxford.
Cal. pat. rolls Ire., Jas I	*Irish patent rolls of James I: facsimile of the Irish record commissioners' calendar prepared prior to 1830*, with foreword by M.C. Griffith (Dublin, 1966).
Carew MSS	*Calendar of the Carew manuscripts preserved in the archiepiscopal library at Lambeth 1515–74* [etc.] (6 vols, London, 1867–73).
CSPI	*Calendar of state papers relating to Ireland* (24 vols, London, 1860–1912).
Fiants Ire.	*The Irish fiants of the Tudor sovereigns, 1521–1603* (4 vols, Dublin, 1994).
IHS	*Irish Historical Studies.*
MS	Manuscript.
NAI	National Archives of Ireland.
New History of Ireland	T.W. Moody, F.X. Martin and F.J. Byrne (eds), *A new history of Ireland, iii: early modern Ireland, 1534–1691* (Oxford, 1976).
NHI	*A new history of Ireland.*
ODNB	*Oxford dictionary of national biography.*
TNA	The National Archives, London.
SP	State Papers.
TCD	Trinity College Dublin.
Valor beneficiorum	*Valor beneficiorum ecclesiasticorum in Hibernia* (Dublin, 1741).

INTRODUCTION

1 He then became known as Sir John O'Reilly: Ciaran Brady, 'The end of the O'Reilly lordship, 1584–1610' in David Edwards (ed.), *Regions and rulers in Ireland, 1100–1650* (Dublin, 2004), pp 174–200 at p. 179.

2 Bernadette Cunningham, 'The anglicisation of east Breifne: the O'Reillys and the emergence of Co. Cavan' in Raymond Gillespie (ed.), *Cavan: essays on the history of an Irish county* (2nd ed., Dublin, 2004), pp 51–72, 202–4 at pp 51, 59.

3 TNA, SP 63/117/7; *CSPI, 1574–85*, p. 320; Cunningham, 'The anglicisation of east Breifne', p. 62.

4 TNA, SP 63/177/42; TNA, SP 63/175/5; TNA, SP 63/176/60; TNA, SP 63/178/53; TNA, SP 63/178/65.

5 Cunningham, 'The anglicisation of east Breifne', pp 69–70.

6 TNA, SP 63/200/98; TNA, SP 63/200/129; TNA, SP 63/200/137.

7 Cunningham, 'The anglicisation of east Breifne', p. 71.

8 TNA, SP 63/207(ii)/122; TNA, SP 63/207(vi)/46; TNA, SP 63/207(vi)/66; TNA, SP 63/208(i)/38.

9 *CSPI, 1601–3*, pp 135–6, 454, 524; *Fiants Ire., Eliz.*, no. 6657.

10 Brady, 'The end of the O'Reilly lordship, 1584–1610', pp 188–9.

11 *CSPI, 1603–06*, p. 565.

12 G.A. Hayes-McCoy, 'Sir John Davies in Cavan in 1606 and 1610' in *Breifne*, 3 (1960), pp 177–91 at pp 183, 185–6.

13 H. Morley (ed.), *Ireland under Elizabeth and James I* (London, 1890), pp 384–7; Brady, 'The end of the O'Reilly lordship, 1584–1610', pp 175–6.

1. PLANTATION IN CAVAN, 1609–41

1 For what follows, see Philip Robinson, *The plantation of Ulster* (Dublin, 1984).

2 George Hill, *An historical account of the plantation in Ulster* (Belfast, 1877; repr. Shannon, 1970), p. 458.

3 William J. Smyth, *Map-making, landscapes and memory: a geography of colonial and early modern Ireland, c.1530–1750* (Cork, 2006), p. 70.

4 Raymond Gillespie, 'The end of an era: Ulster and the outbreak of the 1641 rising' in Ciaran Brady and Raymond Gillespie (eds), *Natives and newcomers: the making of Irish colonial society, 1534–1641* (Dublin, 1986), pp 191–213 at p. 194; R.J. Hunter, 'The English undertakers in the plantation of Ulster 1610–41' in *Breifne*, 16 (1973–5), pp 471–500 at p. 471. The Church of Ireland received 6500 acres in Cavan: Hill, *An historical account of the plantation in Ulster*, pp 112–13.

5 Smyth, *Map-making, landscapes and memory*, pp 66–9.

6 R.J. Hunter, 'An Ulster plantation town – Virginia' in *Breifne*, 13 (1970), pp 43–51 at p. 43.

7 Hunter, 'An Ulster plantation town – Virginia', p. 46.

8 Ibid., pp 47–8.

9 Hill, *An historical account of the plantation in Ulster*, p. 457.

10 Ibid., pp 457–8. For more on Benjamin Culme, see: Hugh O'Reilly, 'Lisnamaine castle' in *Breifne*, 23 (1985), pp 263–77 at p. 271.

11 Hunter, 'An Ulster plantation town – Virginia', p. 49.

12 P. Ó Gallachair, '1622 survey of Cavan' in *Breifne*, 1 (1958), pp 60–75 at p. 64. This document has been republished with corrections in Victor Treadwell (ed.), *The Irish commission of 1622: an investigation of the Irish administration 1615–22 and its consequences 1623–24* (Dublin, 2006), pp 510–23.

13 Ó Gallachair, '1622 survey of Cavan', pp 63–4.

14 Quoted from T.S. Smyth, *The civic history of the town of Cavan* (Dublin, 1938), p. 18.

15 Ibid., pp 20, 40.

16 Treadwell, *The Irish commission of 1622*, p. 523.

17 Hill, *An historical account of the plantation in Ulster*, p. 467.

18 Also known as Francis, Hamilton shall be referred to as Frederick throughout this book for the sake of continuity.

19 Hill, *An historical account of the plantation in Ulster*, p. 469; Ó Gallachair, '1622 survey of Cavan', pp 72–3.

20 *CSPI, 1608–10*, p. 489; T.W. Moody, 'Ulster plantation papers' in *Anal. Hib.*, 8 (1938), pp 180–297; Ó Gallachair, '1622 survey of Cavan', p. 69.

21 *CSPI, 1611–14*, p. 128; *Cal. Carew MSS, 1603–24*, p. 227; Hill, *An historical account of the plantation in Ulster*, pp 464–5.

22 Hill, *An historical account of the plantation in Ulster*, pp 464–5.

23 Hunter, 'The English undertakers in the plantation', p. 480.

24 Ibid., p. 465.

25 Ó Gallachair, '1622 survey of Cavan', p. 69.

26 Hunter, 'The English undertakers in the plantation', pp 491–2.

27 Pádraig Lenihan, *Confederate Catholics at war, 1641–49* (Cork, 2001), p. 53.

28 E.S. Shuckburgh (ed.), *Two biographies of William Bedell, bishop of Kilmore; with a selection of his letters and an unpublished treatise* (Cambridge, 1902), p. 190.

29 Treadwell, *The Irish commission of 1622*, pp 515–16.

30 R.J. Hunter & Michael Perceval-Maxwell, 'The muster roll of c.1630: Co. Cavan' in *Breifne*, 18 (1977–8), pp 206–22 at pp 208–10; idem, 'The

English undertakers in the plantation',
p. 488.

31 *CSPI, 1611–14*, p. 334; R.J. Hunter,
'Towns in the Ulster plantation' in
Studia Hibernica, 11 (1971), pp 40–79 at
p. 74.

32 Hill, *An historical account of the plantation
in Ulster*, pp 465–6.

33 Hunter, 'The English undertakers in
the plantation', p. 479; Ó Gallachair,
'1622 survey of Cavan', p. 69.

34 Robinson, *The plantation of Ulster*,
pp 154–5.

35 Ó Gallachair, '1622 survey of Cavan',
p. 69; Hunter, 'The English undertakers
in the plantation', p. 483.

36 Gillespie, 'The end of an era', p. 195;
For maps detailing land ownership in
early seventeenth-century Cavan, see
P.J. Duffy, 'Perspectives on the making
of the Cavan landscape' in Gillespie
(ed.), *Cavan*, pp 14–36 at pp 22, 24.

37 Raymond Gillespie, *The transformation
of the Irish economy, 1550–1700*, Studies
in Irish economic and social history, 6
(Dundalk, 1991), pp 4, 25.

38 Brady, 'The end of the O'Reilly
lordship, 1584–1610', pp 185–7.

39 Raymond Gillespie, 'Harvest crises in
early seventeenth-century Ireland' in
Irish Economic and Social History, 11
(1984), pp 5–18; idem, *The
transformation of the Irish economy*;
Nicholas Canny, *Making Ireland British,
1580–1650* (Oxford, 2001), p. 473.

40 Nicholas Canny, 'What really
happened in 1641?' in Jane Ohlmeyer
(ed.), *Ireland: from independence to
occupation, 1641–1660* (Cambridge,
1995), pp 24–42 at p. 31; Gillespie, 'The
end of an era', pp 195, 199.

41 *CSPI, 1615–25*, p. 480; Hunter, 'The
English undertakers in the plantation',
pp 491–2.

42 *CSPI, 1625–32*, pp 35–6, 220, 468. It
would be unwise to take these reports
at face value, as representatives of the
county were petitioning for less severe
cess exactions. Moreover, food was
described as being in abundant supply
and being 'sold at an absurdly low
price' in 1646: 'My Irish campaign' in
Catholic Bulletin, 7 (1917), pp 111–14,
179–82, 246–9, 295–6 at p. 249.

43 Calendar of Exchequer Inquisitions,
Ulster (NAI, RC 5/25, ff 121–2).

44 Deposition of Arnold Cosby (TCD,
MS 833, ff 124–5).

45 Deposition of Richard Parsons (TCD,
MS 832, f. 88); Brian Mac Cuarta, 'The
plantation of Leitrim, 1620–41' in *IHS*,
32 (2001), pp 297–320 at p. 317;
Hunter, 'The English undertakers in
the plantation', p. 491.

46 Ó Gallachair, '1622 survey of Cavan',
p. 69; Hunter, 'The English undertakers
in the plantation', p. 491; idem, 'Towns
in the Ulster plantation', p. 71.

47 Ó Gallachair, '1622 survey of Cavan',
p. 69; Robinson, *Plantation of Ulster*, p.
144; Hunter, 'Towns in the Ulster
plantation', p. 75.

48 Shuckburgh (ed.), *Two biographies of
William Bedell*, p. 57; Hunter, 'The
English undertakers in the plantation',
p. 491.

49 Canny, *Making Ireland British*, p. 348.

50 *CSPI, 1608–10*, p. 55; Moody, 'Ulster
plantation papers', p. 281; Hill, *An
historical account of the plantation in
Ulster*, p. 113.

51 Deposition of Richard Parsons (TCD,
MS 832, f. 90).

52 Indeed, it had been suggested in the
1590s that boats be located at
Belturbet as a means of controlling
access into Ulster: Raymond Gillespie,
'Faith, family and fortune: the
structures of everyday life in early
modern Cavan' in Gillespie (ed.),
Cavan, pp 99–114 at pp 101–2.

53 Robinson, *Plantation of Ulster*, p. 174.

54 *CSPI, 1611–14*, p. 128; *Cal. Carew MSS,
1603–24*, p. 227.

55 Hunter, 'The English undertakers in
the plantation', p. 479.

56 Ibid., p. 480; O'Reilly, 'Lisnamaine
castle', pp 263–4.

57 Hunter, 'The English undertakers in
the plantation', p. 496.

58 Deposition of William Gibbs (TCD,
MS 832, f. 140); deposition of William
Atwood (TCD, MS 832, f. 102);
Robinson, *The plantation of Ulster*, p. 173;
Hunter, 'The English undertakers in
the plantation', pp 491–2, 496.

59 Cal. pat. rolls Ire., Jas. I, p. 261.
60 Deposition of Richard Parsons (TCD, MS 832, f. 91).

2. RELIGION IN CAVAN, 1609–41

1 Brian McCabe, 'An Elizabethan prelate: John Garvey' in Breifne, 26 (1988), pp 594–604; Colm Lennon, 'The Nugent family and the diocese of Kilmore in the sixteenth and early seventeenth centuries' in Breifne, 37 (2001), pp 360–74.
2 Charles McNeill (ed.), 'The Perrot papers' in Anal. Hib., 12 (1943), pp 1–66 at p. 11.
3 According to Alan Ford, 'The reformation in Kilmore before 1641' in Gillespie (ed.), Cavan, pp 73–98 at p. 78. It has been claimed, however, that James Plunkett was vicar-general of Kilmore, at least from 1618: Philip O'Connell, The diocese of Kilmore: its history and antiquities (Dublin, 1937), pp 394–5.
4 Although provided to the see of Kilmore in 1625, O'Reilly was not actually consecrated as bishop there until 1626: ODNB, sv, 'Hugh O'Reilly'.
5 Ignatius Fennessy, 'Richard Brady OFM, bishop of Kilmore, 1580–1607' in Breifne, 36 (2000), pp 225–42 at p. 235.
6 O'Connell, The diocese of Kilmore, p. 396; Francis J. MacKiernan, 'The Franciscan friary in Cavan' in Breifne, 35 (1999), pp 85–102 at p. 96.
7 Fiants Ire., Elizabeth, nos 1681, 4025, 4923; O'Connell, The diocese of Kilmore, pp 185–6; Raymond Gillespie, 'Relics, reliquaries and hagiography in south Ulster, 1450–1550' in Rachel Moss, Colmán Ó Clabaigh OSB and Salvador Ryan (eds), Art and devotion in late medieval Ireland (Dublin, 2006), pp 184–201 at pp 191–2; Brendan Scott, Religion and reformation in the Tudor diocese of Meath (Dublin, 2006), p. 123.
8 Séamus P. Ó Mórdha, 'Hugh O'Reilly (1581?–1653): a reforming prelate' in

Breifne, 13 (1970), pp 1–42 at p. 21; O'Connell, The diocese of Kilmore, pp 408–9; Massari, 'My Irish campaign', p. 247.
9 Tadhg Ó hAnnracháin, Catholic reformation in Ireland: the mission of Rinuccini 1645–1649 (Oxford, 2002), pp 42–3.
10 O'Connell, The diocese of Kilmore, p. 406.
11 Ó hAnnracháin, Catholic reformation in Ireland, p. 45.
12 John Hagan (ed.), 'Miscellanea Vaticano-Hibernica' in Archiv. Hib., 5 (1916), p. 81.
13 Lenihan, Confederate Catholics at war, p. 37; Shuckburgh (ed.), Two biographies of William Bedell, pp 297, 300; MacKiernan, 'The Franciscan friary in Cavan', p. 97; J.T. Gilbert, A contemporary history of affairs in Ireland from 1641–1652 (3 vols, Dublin, 1879), iii, 479; Charles McNeill (ed.), The Tanner letters (Dublin, 1943), p. 104.
14 Massari, 'My Irish campaign', pp 247–8.
15 O'Connell, The diocese of Kilmore, pp 422–3.
16 Ibid., p. 424; Rory Masterson, 'The diocese of Kilmore and the priory of Fore: 1000–1540' in Breifne, 39 (2003), pp 1–20 at p. 6.
17 It is even possible that the bishop was imprisoned for refusing to appear before the court, but this is not known for sure: O'Connell, The diocese of Kilmore, p. 426.
18 O'Connell, The diocese of Kilmore, p. 426.
19 Ó hAnnracháin, Catholic reformation in Ireland, pp 43, 46.
20 Deposition of George Creighton (TCD, MS 832, ff 150–6); Francis J. MacKiernan, 'Thomas Fitzsimons (1614–80)' in Breifne, 37 (2001), pp 313–35 at p. 315; Shuckburgh (ed.), Two biographies of William Bedell, p. 204.
21 David Edwards, 'A haven of popery: English Catholic migration to Ireland in the age of plantations' in Alan Ford and John McCafferty (eds), The origins of sectarianism in early modern Ireland (Cambridge, 2005), pp 95–126 at p. 119.
22 TCD, MS 550, ff 142–3.

23 Called 'Hanna' in the manuscript:
    TCD, MS 550, f. 144.
24 TCD, MS 550, f. 144.
25 Ibid., ff 143–144, 148.
26 Alan Ford, *The Protestant reformation in
    Ireland, 1590–1641* (2nd ed., Dublin,
    1997), p. 195.
27 Aidan Clarke, 'Bishop William Bedell
    (1571–1642) and the Irish reformation'
    in Ciaran Brady (ed.), *Worsted in the
    game: losers in Irish history* (Dublin,
    1989), pp 61–70 at p. 66.
28 Calculated from TCD, MS 550,
    ff 144–53.
29 McNeill (ed.), *The Tanner letters*, p. 90.
    Moyne had only been bishop since
    1625: O'Reilly, 'Lisnamaine castle',
    p. 271.
30 Bodl. MS Rawl., Lett 89, ff 64r–v;
    Terence McCaughey, *Dr Bedell and Mr
    King: the making of the Irish bible*
    (Dublin, 2001), p. 2.
31 Ford, 'The reformation in Kilmore
    before 1641', pp 88–9.
32 *ODNB, s.v.*, 'William Bedell';
    McCaughey, *Dr Bedell and Mr King*, p. 2.
33 Shuckburgh (ed.), *Two biographies of
    William Bedell*, pp 125–6, 129. Land
    had been set aside in Tullyhaw for the
    erection of a free school which had
    not been built by 1622: Treadwell, *The
    Irish commission of 1622*, p. 523.
34 Shuckburgh (ed.), *Two biographies of
    William Bedell*, p. 41.
35 Scott, *Religion and reformation*, p. 57;
    Ford, 'The reformation in Kilmore
    before 1641', p. 76.
36 TCD, MS 550, ff 142–3.
37 Bedell mistakenly believed that the
    gifts of livestock being offered to him
    on his arrival in Cavan were a bribe
    and refused accordingly, inadvertently
    causing great offence: Shuckburgh
    (ed.), *Two biographies of William Bedell*,
    pp 29, 300.
38 Hunter, 'An Ulster plantation town –
    Virginia', p. 49.
39 TCD, MS 550, ff 143–145, 149, 153;
    Shuckburgh (ed.), *Two biographies of
    William Bedell*, p. 57.
40 James Kelly, 'The Catholic church in
    Kilmore, 1580–1880' in Gillespie (ed.),
    Cavan, pp 115–38 at p. 117.
41 Scott, *Religion and reformation*, p. 68.
42 T.C. Mag Uidhir, 'The Cavan
    inquisitions of 1588, 1590 and 1609' in
    Breifne, 28 (1991), pp 272–91 at p. 273.
43 *Valor beneficiorum*, p. 7; O'Connell, *The
    diocese of Kilmore*, pp 403–4.
44 *CSPI, 1633–47*, p. 88.
45 Ford, 'The reformation in Kilmore
    before 1641', p. 80.
46 Shuckburgh (ed.), *Two biographies of
    William Bedell*, pp 45, 332.
47 Colm Lennon & Ciaran Diamond,
    'The ministry of the Church of
    Ireland, 1536–1636' in T.C. Barnard &
    W.G. Neely (eds), *The clergy of the
    Church of Ireland, 1000–2000: messengers,
    watchmen and stewards* (Dublin, 2006),
    pp 44–58 at p. 56.
48 TCD, MS 550, f. 165.
49 O'Connell, *The diocese of Kilmore*,
    p. 424.
50 Ford, 'The reformation in Kilmore
    before 1641', p. 91.
51 Shuckburgh (ed.), *Two biographies of
    William Bedell*, p. xvii; *ODNB, s.v.*,
    'William Bedell'.
52 TCD, MS 550, f. 145; Shuckburgh
    (ed.), *Two biographies of William Bedell*,
    p. 332; Ford, 'The reformation in
    Kilmore before 1641', pp 89, 93.
53 Raymond Gillespie, 'The Church of
    Ireland clergy, c.1640: representation
    and reality' in Barnard & Neely (eds),
    The clergy of the Church of Ireland, pp
    59–77 at pp 61–2.
54 Proposals to redraw the parishes as
    smaller areas went ignored: Ford, 'The
    reformation in Kilmore before 1641',
    p. 80. For a map detailing the parishes
    in Cavan, see P.J. Duffy, 'The shape of
    the parish' in Elizabeth FitzPatrick &
    Raymond Gillespie (eds), *The parish in
    medieval and early modern Ireland:
    community, territory and building* (Dublin,
    2006), pp 33–61 at p. 38.
55 TCD, MS 550, ff 144–53.
56 *CSPI, 1633–47*, p. 206; Shuckburgh
    (ed.), *Two biographies of William Bedell*,
    pp 45, 332.
57 Shuckburgh (ed.), *Two biographies of
    William Bedell*, pp 132, 142–3, 341–2;
    Ford, 'The reformation in Kilmore
    before 1641', pp 91–2.

58 Clarke, 'Bishop William Bedell (1571–1642) and the Irish reformation', p. 67.

59 *CSPI, 1625–32*, p. 481.

60 Shuckburgh (ed.), *Two biographies of William Bedell*, pp 31–2, 302, 311.

61 Ibid., p. 30.

62 Ford, *The Protestant reformation*, pp 208–9.

63 TCD, MS 550, ff 144, 148; C.R. Erlington (ed.), *The whole works of the most Reverend James Ussher* (16 vols, Dublin, 1847), xv, 473–6; Shuckburgh (ed.), *Two biographies of William Bedell*, p. 302.

64 Shuckburgh (ed.), *Two biographies of William Bedell*, pp 51, 121–3; Aidan Clarke, *The Old English in Ireland* (London, 1966), pp 256, 260.

3. THE 1641 RISING IN CAVAN

1 Gillespie, 'The end of an era', p. 202; Clarke, 'The genesis of the Ulster rising of 1641', p. 35.

2 Allan I. MacInnes, *The British revolution, 1629–1660* (Basingstoke, 2005), pp 130–46. For recent, in-depth accounts of the events leading up to the rising, see: Michael Perceval-Maxwell, *The outbreak of the Irish rebellion of 1641* (Dublin, 1994); Aidan Clarke, 'The genesis of the Ulster rising of 1641' in Peter Roebuck (ed.), *Plantation to partition* (Belfast, 1981), pp 29–45; Nicholas Canny, 'Religion, politics and the Irish rising of 1641' in Judith Devlin and Ronan Fanning (eds), *Religion and rebellion: historical studies*, xx (Dublin, 1997), pp 40–70.

3 Deposition of Marmaduke Batemanson (TCD, MS 832, f. 80); Gillespie, 'The end of an era', p. 201.

4 Deposition of Thomas Taylor (TCD, MS 833, f. 70); *CSPI, 1633–47*, pp 347–8; Gillespie, 'The end of an era', p. 203; Clarke, 'The genesis of the Ulster rising of 1641', p. 35; idem, *The Old English in Ireland*, p. 168.

5 Canny, *Making Ireland British*, p. 472.

6 Joseph Cope, 'The experience of survival during the 1641 Irish

7 David A. O'Hara, *English newsbooks and Irish rebellion, 1641–1649* (Dublin, 2006), pp 28–54. There are a number of examples of these illustrations in Brian Mac Cuarta (ed.), *Ulster 1641: aspects of the rising* (Belfast, 1993).

8 Perceval-Maxwell, *The outbreak of the Irish rebellion*, p. 213; Jane Ohlmeyer, *Civil war and restoration in the three Stuart kingdoms: the career of Randal MacDonnell, marquis of Antrim, 1609–83* (Cambridge, 1993), pp 10–17, 77–102.

9 Clarke, 'The 1641 depositions', p. 112; Michael Perceval-Maxwell, 'The Ulster rising of 1641 and the depositions' in *IHS*, 21 (1978), pp 144–67.

10 Nicholas Canny, *Kingdom and colony: Ireland in the Atlantic world, 1560–1800* (Baltimore, 1988), p. 96; David Hume, *The history of Great Britain, Volume I, containing the reigns of James I and Charles I* (Edinburgh, 1754), p. 100; J.M. Barkley, *A short history of the Presbyterian church in Ireland* (Belfast, 1959), p. 10; Clarke, 'The 1641 depositions', p. 111.

11 For some examples, see Brendan Scott, 'The 1641 rising in the plantation town of Belturbet' in *Breifne*, 40 (2004), pp 155–75, fn. 11. See also T.C. Barnard, '1641: a bibliographical essay' in Mac Cuarta (ed.), *Ulster 1641*, pp 173–86; Canny, *Making Ireland British*, pp 461–9.

12 Mary Hickson (ed.), *Ireland in the seventeenth century; or, The Irish massacres of 1641–2* (2 vols, London, 1884); T. Crofton Croker (ed.), *Narratives illustrative of the contests in Ireland in 1641 and 1698* (London, 1841); J.P. Mahaffy, *An epoch in Irish history, 1591 to 1660* (London, 1903); E.W. Hamilton, *The Irish rebellion of 1641; with a history of the events which led up to and succeeded it* (London, 1920). See Barnard, '1641: a bibliographical essay'.

13 W.E.H. Lecky, *A history of Ireland in the eighteenth century* (5 vols, new ed. London, 1892), i, 1–111; Thomas Fitzpatrick, *The bloody bridge; and other papers relating to the insurrection of 1641* (Dublin, 1903).

rebellion' in *Historical Journal*, 46 (2003), pp 295–316 at p. 296.

4 Some historians who have been making use of the depositions recently include: Canny, 'What really happened in 1641?'; idem, *Making Ireland British*, pp 461–550; Gillespie, 'The end of an era'; idem, 'Destabilizing Ulster, 1641–2' in Mac Cuarta (ed.), *Ulster 1641*, pp 107–21; Simms, 'Violence in Co. Armagh 1641'; Brian Mac Cuarta, 'Anti-Protestantism in south Ulster 1641–2: the evidence of the 1641 depositions' (unpublished MPhil. thesis, Trinity College, Dublin, 1994).

5 Nicholas Canny, 'The 1641 depositions as a source for the writing of social and economic history: Co. Cork as a case study' in Patrick O'Flanagan and Cornelius Buttimer (eds), *Cork: history and society* (Dublin, 1993), pp 249–308.

6 Idem, 'What really happened in 1641?', pp 25–7.

7 Formerly known as Miles, O'Reilly reverted to the Gaelicized Mulmore at the beginning of the rising: Perceval-Maxwell, *The outbreak of the Irish rising of 1641*, p. 220.

8 Ibid., p. 220; Hickson, *Ireland in the seventeenth century*, p. 311; Gilbert (ed.), *A contemporary history of affairs in Ireland from 1641–52* (3 vols, Dublin, 1879), iii, 478–9.

9 Deposition of Joanne Woods the younger (TCD, MS 832, f. 166); deposition of Henry Baxter (TCD, MS 832, f. 81).

10 Ó Gallacháir, '1622 survey of Cavan', 69; Hickson, *Ireland in the seventeenth century*, ii, p. 309.

11 Hickson, *Ireland in the seventeenth century*, ii, 309; Cope, 'The experience of survival', pp 303–5.

12 Deposition of Philip Ward (TCD, MS 832, f. 101); deposition of John Anderson (TCD, MS 833, f. 98).

13 Deposition of Richard Lewis (TCD, MS 833, f. 34); *CSPI, 1633–47*, p. 348.

14 Deposition of Elizabeth Woodhouse (TCD, MS 833, f. 90).

15 Deposition of Henry Baxter (TCD, MS 832, f. 81); deposition of Thomas Taylor (TCD, MS 832, f. 98).

16 Deposition of John Anderson (TCD,

MS 832, f. 98); Clarke, *The Old English in Ireland*, pp 256, 260.

27 Deposition of John Whitman (TCD, MS 832, f. 57); Gilbert (ed.), *A contemporary history of affairs in Ireland*, iii, 479–80.

28 Cope, 'The experience of survival', p. 300.

29 Deposition of John Heron (TCD, MS 832, ff 101–2; TCD, MS 833, f. 6); deposition of Adam Glover (TCD, MS 833, f. 1); deposition of John Hickman (TCD, MS 832, f. 142).

30 Gilbert (ed.), *A contemporary history of affairs in Ireland*, iii, 485–6.

31 Shuckburgh (ed.), *Two biographies of William Bedell*, pp 59–61, 176.

32 Deposition of Henry Woke (TCD, MS 832, f. 138); deposition of Thomas Taylor (TCD, MS 832, f. 98). The strippings do not seem to have been primarily sexual in motivation. There were no reported instances of rape in Cavan during the rising and relatively few throughout Ireland. Rather, the strippings seemed to fulfil a social function, demeaning the Protestants for all to see. Their clothes were also valuable in themselves: Canny, *Making Ireland British*, pp 542–5; Simms, 'Violence in Co. Armagh 1641', p. 136.

33 Deposition of Philip Ward (TCD, MS 832, f. 101).

34 Hickson, *Ireland in the seventeenth century*, ii, 389. It has been suggested that Creighton may have exaggerated these figures: Cope, 'The experience of survival', p. 307.

35 Deposition of Thomas Woodward (TCD, MS 832, f. 135); Cope, 'The experience of survival', p. 307.

36 Deposition of Richard Lewis (TCD, MS 832, ff 45, 87).

37 Deposition of William Atwood (TCD, MS 832, f. 102).

38 Deposition of Edward Philpott (TCD, MS 832, f. 72).

39 Canny, *Making Ireland British*, p. 476.

40 Deposition of Nataniel Clark (TCD, MS 833, f. 225); deposition of John Irwin (TCD, MS 832, f. 139).

41 Deposition of Thomas Dennibers (TCD, MS 833, f. 75).

42 Deposition of Ambrose Bedell (TCD, MS 833, f. 105).

43 Shuckburgh (ed.), *Two biographies of William Bedell*, pp 61–2.

44 Ibid., pp 65, 189; *ODNB, s.v.*, 'William Bedell'.

45 Deposition of Arthur Culme (TCD, MS 832, ff 115–9); Shuckburgh (ed.), *Two biographies of William Bedell*, pp 66–7, 190; *ODNB, s.v.*, 'William Bedell'. Culme, who had failed to arm himself before the outbreak of this rising, was not to make the same mistake twice; he joined the Cromwellian army, rising to the position of colonel and died at Clonmel in 1650: O'Reilly, 'Lisnamaine castle', pp 270–1.

46 Shuckburgh (ed.), *Two biographies of William Bedell*, pp 69–73; J.G. Simms, 'Denis Sheridan and some of his descendants' in *Breifne*, 16 (1973–5), pp 460–70 at pp 461–2. Bedell was seventy when he died, not seventy-two, as has been claimed: *ODNB, s.v.*, 'William Bedell'; Clarke, 'Bishop William Bedell (1571–1642) and the Irish reformation', p. 68.

47 Shuckburgh (ed.), *Two biographies of William Bedell*, pp 73–5, 205.

48 Deposition of Philip Ward (TCD, MS 832, ff 60, 100); deposition of William Gibbs (TCD, MS 832, f. 140); deposition of Thomas Smith (TCD, MS 832, f. 143).

49 Deposition of William Gibbs (TCD, MS 832, f. 140); Shuckburgh (ed.), *Two biographies of William Bedell*, p. 191; Hickson, *Ireland in the seventeenth century*, p. 306; Canny, *Making Ireland British*, p. 477.

50 The dating of this event poses some difficulties; Richard Parsons, whose wife was from Belturbet, dates it to 14 January 1642, and Brian Mac Cuarta also dates it to mid-January. Richard Bennett, a captive in the town at the time, however, places the massacre in May 1642. As Gibbs was one of those attacked, however, it is likely that his dating of 30 January 1642 is more accurate: deposition of William Gibbs (TCD, MS 832, f. 140); deposition of

Richard Parsons (TCD, MS 832, f. 89); deposition of Richard Bennett (TCD, MS 832, f. 81); Mac Cuarta, 'Anti-Protestantism in south Ulster 1641–2', pp 80–2.

51 Deposition of William Bloxton (TCD, MS 832, f. 85).

52 Deposition of William Gibbs (TCD, MS 832, f. 140); Hickson, *Ireland in the seventeenth century*, ii, 303–5.

53 Gibbs' misfortunes had not yet ended. Three of his children died in captivity and when he, his wife and one surviving child finally left Belturbet in June 1642, they were stripped of their clothes four miles from Kells: deposition of William Gibbs (TCD, MS 832, f. 140).

54 Donnell O'Reilly's scope for clemency was limited. It was alleged that he ignored the pleas of mercy made upon her knees by one Widow Munday and forced her into the river to her death: Hickson, *Ireland in the seventeenth century*, ii, 304.

55 Deposition of William Gibbs (TCD, MS 832, f. 140); Hickson, *Ireland in the seventeenth century*, ii, 303–4.

56 Deposition of William Gibbs (TCD, MS 832, f. 140).

57 Canny, 'What really happened in 1641?', p. 28.

58 The families of James Carr and Timothy Dickson were among those who were drowned: deposition of William Gibbs (TCD, MS 832, f. 140); Hickson, *Ireland in the seventeenth century*, ii, 303–4. Some of those who drowned may have been from Leitrim, which would explain why Kirkeber and Gibbs were unable to name them: Canny, *Making Ireland British*, p. 494. For the names of those who were drowned in Belturbet, see appendices.

59 The following are just a selection of the deponents who gave various estimates of unnamed people drowned in Belturbet even though they were not eyewitnesses: deposition of William Jameson (TCD, MS 832, f. 63; TCD, MS 833, f. 161); deposition of Marmaduke Batemanson (TCD, MS 832, f. 80); deposition of Richard

Parsons (TCD, MS 832, f. 90); deposition of John Watson (TCD, MS 832, f. 111); deposition of John Hickman (TCD, MS 832, f. 142; TCD, MS 833, f. 156); deposition of William North (TCD, MS 833, f. 179).

60 Deposition of Richard Bennett (TCD, MS 832, f. 81); Hickson, *Ireland in the seventeenth century*, ii, 304, 306.

61 Deposition of Thomas Crant (TCD, MS 832, f. 74); deposition of James Mardoghe (TCD, MS 832, f. 110); Mac Cuarta, 'Anti-Protestantism in south Ulster 1641–2', pp 11, 15, 79.

62 Deposition of John Anderson (TCD, MS 832, f. 68; TCD, MS 833, f. 98). For more on the rising in Leitrim and Fermanagh, see: Daniel Gallogly, '1641 rebellion in Leitrim' in *Breifne*, 8 (1966), pp 441–54; Raymond Gillespie, 'The murder of Arthur Champion and the rising of 1641 in Fermanagh' in *Clogher Record*, 14 (1993), pp 52–66.

63 Deposition of Marmaduke Batemanson (TCD, MS 832, f. 80).

64 Canny, *Making Ireland British*, p. 484; Mac Cuarta (ed.), *Ulster 1641*, p. xiii.

65 Deposition of Marmaduke Batemanson (TCD, MS 832, f. 80).

66 Deposition of Richard Bennett (TCD, MS 832, f. 81); deposition of William Jameson (TCD, MS 832, f. 64; TCD, MS 833, f. 161); Hickson, *Ireland in the seventeenth century*, ii, 304.

67 Deposition of Richard Bennett (TCD, MS 832, f. 81); Hickson, *Ireland in the seventeenth century*, ii, 306. Nevertheless, some of those responsible claimed that they had O'Reilly's permission for what they did: deposition of Thomas Smith (TCD, MS 832, f. 143).

68 Hunter & Perceval-Maxwell, 'The muster roll of *c.*1630', p. 222.

69 Quoted in Robert Armstrong, *Protestant war: the 'British' of Ireland and the wars of the three kingdoms* (Manchester, 2005), pp 29, 33; 'Relation of Henry Jones', p. 487; Daniel Gallogly, 'Sir Frederick Hamilton' in *Breifne*, 9 (1966), pp 55–99.

70 Deposition of Thomas Crant (TCD, MS 832, f. 74).

71 Deposition of Ambrose Bedell (TCD, MS 833, f. 105); Lenihan, *Confederate Catholics at war*, p. 35.

72 Shuckburgh (ed.), *Two biographies of William Bedell*, p. 211.

73 Clarke, *The Old English in Ireland*, pp 165, 167–8.

74 R. Dunlop, 'The forged commission of 1641' in *English Historical Review*, 2 (1887), pp 527–33. It seems that Philip MacMulmore O'Reilly later quarrelled with his nephew Mulmore and others over the authenticity of the seal and was imprisoned for a short time: deposition of Elizabeth Woodhouse (TCD, MS 833, f. 90); deposition of Richard Castledine (TCD, MS 832, f. 124); Cope, 'The experience of survival', pp 300–2.

75 *CSPI, 1633–47*, pp 347–8; Shuckburgh (ed.), *Two biographies of William Bedell*, p. 178.

76 Clarke, *The Old English in Ireland*, p. 168; Canny, *Making Ireland British*, pp 440–1; Shuckburgh (ed.), *Two biographies of William Bedell*, p. 66.

77 Deposition of John McKewne (TCD, MS 832, f. 71).

78 Deposition of Edward Denman (TCD, MS 832, f. 65); deposition of John Anderson (TCD, MS 832, f. 68); deposition of Thomas Taylor (TCD, MS 832, f. 98); deposition of Adam Glover (TCD, MS 833, f. 1); deposition of Frances and Thomas Lovett (TCD, MS 833, f. 24).

79 Deposition of Nicholas Michael (TCD, MS 832, f. 104); deposition of William Waters (TCD, MS 832, f. 114; TCD, MS 833, f. 200); deposition of John Watson (TCD, MS 832, f. 111).

80 Deposition of Thomas Taylor (TCD, MS 832, f. 98).

81 Deposition of Martin Little (TCD, MS 832, f. 84).

82 Deposition of Richard Parsons (TCD, MS 832, ff 88–92).

83 Deposition of Elizabeth Poke (TCD, MS 833, f. 256).

84 Deposition of Henry Baxter (TCD, MS 832, f. 81).

85 Deposition of William Sharpe (TCD, MS 832, f. 84).

86 Deposition of James Stewart (TCD, MS 832, f. 72); deposition of Martin Little (TCD, MS 832, f. 84); deposition of James Mardoghe (TCD, MS 832, f. 110); deposition of William Reynold (TCD, MS 832, f. 127).

87 Phil Kilroy, 'Radical religion in Ireland, 1641–1660' in Ohlmeyer (ed.), *Ireland: from independence to occupation, 1641–1660*, pp 201–17.

88 Deposition of Richard Lewis of Belturbet (TCD, MS 833, f. 34).

89 Deposition of Thomas Taylor (TCD, MS 833, f. 70); deposition of William Watters (TCD, MS 832, f. 114; TCD, MS 833, f. 200); deposition of Thomas Crant (TCD, MS 832, ff 74, 212).

90 Deposition of Henry Reynolds (TCD, MS 832, f. 62; TCD, MS 833, f. 57). Rumours of this nature were rife across Ulster at this time: Gillespie, 'The end of an era', pp 202–3.

91 Deposition of Thomas Crant (TCD, MS 832, f. 74).

92 Deposition of William Hoe (TCD, MS 832, f. 135).

93 Deposition of John Anderson (TCD, MS 832, f. 68); deposition of Richard Parsons (TCD, MS 832, f. 91).

94 Deposition of John McSkemeine (TCD, MS 832, f. 110; TCD, MS 833, f. 187); deposition of William Watters (TCD, MS 832, f. 114; TCD, MS 833, f. 200).

95 Deposition of James Stewart (TCD, MS 832, f. 72); deposition of Simon Gream (TCD, MS 832, f. 106); deposition of Arthur Culme (TCD, MS 832, f. 115); deposition of William Sharpe (TCD, MS 832 f. 84); Clodagh Tait, 'Using and abusing the dying and the dead in early modern Ireland' in *History Ireland*, 13/1 (2005), pp 16–20 at p. 20. Protestants who died in Cavan at this time were normally buried in unconsecrated fields: deposition of Jane Cuthbertson (TCD, MS 832, f. 141).

96 Deposition of James Mardoghe (TCD, MS 832, ff 110, 112; TCD, MS 833, f. 174); deposition of James Stewart (TCD, MS 832, f. 72).

97 Deposition of Audrey Carington (TCD, MS 832, f. 109).

98 Deposition of Arthur Culme (TCD, MS 832, ff 115–9).

99 Deposition of William Cole (TCD, MS 832, f. 87); deposition of George Creighton (TCD, MS 833, f. 227).

1 Deposition of Thomas Taylor (TCD, MS 832, f. 98).

2 Kelly, 'The Catholic church in Kilmore, 1580–1880', p. 118.

3 Gallogly, '1641 rising in Leitrim', pp 444–5.

4 Deposition of John Whitman (TCD, MS 832, f. 58); deposition of Henry Reynolds (TCD, MS 832, f. 62); Canny, 'What really happened in 1641?', pp 40–1.

5 Canny, 'What really happened in 1641?', pp 38–9; idem, *Making Ireland British*, p. 513; Mac Cuarta, 'Anti-Protestantism in South Ulster 1641–2', pp 16–20.

6 Deposition of John Whitman (TCD, MS 832, f. 58); deposition of Alexander Lord (TCD, MS 832, f. 95); deposition of Thomas Tailor (TCD, MS 832, f. 60); deposition of John Perkins (TCD, MS 832, f. 65); deposition of William Hoe (TCD, MS 832, f. 135).

7 Deposition of John Anderson (TCD, MS 832, f. 69); deposition of Arthur Culme (TCD, MS 832, f. 117).

8 Deposition of Thomas Crant (TCD, MS 832 f. 74). It is possible that this minister was Richard Parsons, who, perhaps understandably, does not mention this in his own deposition: deposition of Richard Parsons (TCD, MS 832, ff 88–90).

9 Deposition of George Creighton (TCD, MS 832, ff 150–6).

10 Deposition of Elizabeth Poke (TCD, MS 833, f. 256).

11 Deposition of Ambrose Bedell (TCD, MS 832, f. 122); Cope, 'The experience of survival', p. 309.

12 Deposition of John McKeown (TCD, MS 832, f. 71); deposition of William King (TCD, MS 832, f. 103); deposition of George Cooke (TCD, MS 832, f. 105); deposition of John McSkemeine (TCD, MS 832, f. 110; TCD, MS 833, f. 187); deposition of Musgrave Arrington (TCD, MS 832, f. 134).

13 Micheál Ó Siochrú, *Confederate Ireland, 1642–1649: a constitutional and political analysis* (Dublin, 1999), p. 187.

14 Canny, *Making Ireland British*, p. 476; idem, 'What really happened in 1641?', p. 32; Gillespie, 'The end of an era', pp 211–12.

15 Canny, *Making Ireland British*, p. 476.

16 Ibid., pp 359, 492.

17 Deposition of Edward Philpott (TCD, MS 832, f. 72). The Butler family did return to Belturbet following the cessation of hostilities in 1653, and continued to play a prominent role in the area before being elevated to the peerage as earls of Lanesborough in the eighteenth century: Anthony Malcolmson, 'The Erne family, estate and archive, *c.*1610–*c.*1950' in E.M. Murphy and W.J. Roulston (eds), *Fermanagh: history and society* (Dublin, 2004), pp 203–39 at p. 207.

18 Deposition of John Heron (TCD, MS 832, ff 101–2; TCD, MS 833, f. 6).

19 Deposition of Edmund Sherwin (TCD, MS 832, f. 97; TCD, MS 833, f. 64).

20 Hunter, 'The English undertakers in the plantation', p. 496.

21 Deposition of William Hoe (TCD, MS 833, f. 11); depositions of Frances and Thomas Lovett (TCD, MS 833, f. 24); deposition of Richard North (TCD, MS 833, f. 41); deposition of John Mioff (TCD, MS 833, f. 83); deposition of Joanne Woods the elder (TCD, MS 833, f. 167). Perhaps it was during this period of uncertainty that a hoard of coins found near Belturbet was buried: Michael Kenny, 'The Deramfield hoard: coin deposited 1641–53' in *Breifne*, 21 (1982), pp 62–75.

22 Deposition of William Gibbs (TCD, MS 832, f. 140); deposition of Henry Baxter (TCD, MS 832, f. 81); deposition of Thomas Smith (TCD, MS 832, f. 143).

23 Of 76 surviving depositions taken for Cavan before 8 March 1642, 74 of them detail their financial losses: Cope, 'The experience of survival', p. 379.

24 Deposition of George Cooke (TCD, MS 832, ff 104–5, 207).

25 Deposition of William Jameson (TCD, MS 832, f. 63); deposition of Thomas Crant (TCD, MS 832, f. 77).

26 O'Connell, *The diocese of Kilmore*, p. 321; MacKiernan, 'The Franciscan friary in Cavan', p. 96.

27 Ó hAnnracháin, *Catholic reformation in Ireland*, p. 50.

28 Cope, 'The experience of survival', pp 304–5.

29 Clarke, 'The genesis of the Ulster rising of 1641', pp 30, 33.

30 Deposition of Richard Castledine (TCD, MS 832, f. 123); deposition of Richard Jackson (TCD, MS 832, f. 130); deposition of George Creighton (TCD, MS 832, f. 146; TCD, MS 833, f. 228).

31 Deposition of George Creighton (TCD, MS 832, f. 146); Shuckburgh (ed.), *Two biographies of William Bedell*, p. 173.

32 Deposition of Richard Parsons (TCD, MS 832, f. 90); Canny, 'What really happened in 1641?', p. 33.

33 Deposition of Marmaduke Batemanson (TCD, MS 832, f. 80); deposition of Martin Little (TCD, MS 832, f. 84); deposition of John McSkemeine (TCD, MS 832, f. 110; TCD, MS 833, f. 187); deposition of William Waters (TCD, MS 832, f. 114; TCD, MS 833, f. 200).

34 Deposition of Richard Parsons (TCD, MS 832, f. 89); deposition of George Creighton (TCD, MS 832, f. 145; TCD, MS 833, f. 227).

35 Deposition of William Jameson (TCD, MS 832, f. 64); deposition of Richard Bennett (TCD, MS 832, f. 81).

36 Deposition of Arthur Culme (TCD, MS 832, ff 115–19).

37 Deposition of George Butterwick (TCD, MS 832, f. 49); Cope, 'The experience of survival', p. 311.

38 Deposition of Ellenor Reinolds (TCD, MS 832, f. 167).

39 Hickson, *Ireland in the seventeenth century*, ii, 304.

40 This protection was limited, as Parsons himself had to go on the run for eighteen months: deposition of Richard Parsons (TCD, MS 832, f. 88).

41 Deposition of George Creighton (TCD, MS 832, f. 149). For more on kinship ties, see Mac Cuarta, 'Anti-Protestantism in south Ulster 1641–2', pp 43–4, 52.

42 Deposition of George Creighton (TCD, MS 832, f. 149).

43 Shuckburgh (ed.), *Two biographies of William Bedell*, p. 190.

44 TCD, MS 550, f. 142; Shuckburgh (ed.), *Two biographies of William Bedell*, p. 70; Ford, 'The reformation in Kilmore before 1641', p. 90.

45 Deposition of John Mioff (TCD, MS 833, f. 83); deposition of Miliford Powell (TCD, MS 833, f. 54); deposition of Mary Ward (TCD, MS 833, f. 80); deposition of Arthur Culme (TCD, MS 832, ff 115–9); Kenny, 'The Deramfield hoard', p. 65; P.J. Corish, 'The Cromwellian conquest, 1649–53' in *New history of Ireland*, iii, 336–52 at 351–2.

46 Gillespie, 'The end of an era', p. 210; Hickson, *Ireland in the seventeenth century*, ii, 183; Mac Cuarta, 'Anti-Protestantism in south Ulster 1641–2', pp 84–8.

47 Deposition of William Jameson (TCD, MS 832, ff 62–4).

48 Deposition of Henry Baxter (TCD, MS 832, f. 81); deposition of Richard Parsons (TCD, MS 832, f. 90).

49 Deposition of John Hickman (TCD, MS 832, f. 142; TCD, MS 833, f. 156).

50 Deposition of Thomas Smith (TCD, MS 832, f. 143); deposition of John Anderson (TCD, MS 832, f. 68; TCD, MS 833, f. 98).

51 Deposition of William Gibbs (TCD, MS 832, f. 140); deposition of John Hickman (TCD, MS 832, f. 142); deposition of Ambrose Bedell (TCD, MS 833, f. 105).

52 Shuckburgh (ed.), *Two biographies of William Bedell*, pp 58–9, 169.

53 J. Salmon, *Bloody news from Ireland* (London, 1641); Canny, 'What really happened in 1641?', p. 31; E.H. Shagan, 'Constructing discord: ideology, propaganda and English responses to the Irish rebellion of 1641' in *Journal of British Studies*, xxxvi (1997), pp 4–34.

54 Raymond Gillespie, 'Imagining angels in early modern Ireland' in Peter Marshall and Alexandra Walsham (eds), *Angels in the early modern world* (Cambridge, 2006), pp 225–32.

55 Cope, 'The experience of survival', p. 307.

56 Gillespie, 'The end of an era', p. 210.

CONCLUSION

1 *ODNB, s.v.*, 'Owen Roe O'Neill'.

2 Jerrold Casway, 'The Ulster refuge of the Northern Army' in *Breifne* (forthcoming).

3 *ODNB, s.v.*, 'Owen Roe O'Neill'; Lenihan, *Confederate Catholics at war*, pp 68, 215–16.

4 Ó Siochrú, *Confederate Ireland*, p. 107.

5 Conleth Manning, 'Clogh Oughter castle' in *Breifne*, 27 (1989–90), pp 20–61 at p. 34.

6 Massari, 'My Irish campaign', p. 246.

7 Ibid., p. 247.

8 Ibid., p. 249.

9 Ó Siochrú, *Confederate Ireland*, p. 118.

10 Kenny, 'The Deramfield hoard', p. 65.

11 Manning, 'Clogh Oughter castle', p. 35; Jerrold Casway, 'Unpublished letters and papers of Owen Roe O'Neill' in *Anal. Hib.*, 29 (1980), pp 220–48 at p. 246; idem, *Owen Roe O'Neill and the struggle for Catholic Ireland* (Philadelphia, 1984), p. 260; idem, 'The Belturbet council and election of March 1650' in *Clogher Record*, 12 (1986), pp 159–170 at p. 159. Rebuilt sometime during the 1630s and situated in a wood, burials had begun to take place in the friary once more. Massari spent a night there in 1646. He described it as 'a marvellous structure in the Ulster fashion, the church, cells, refectory and all other apartments being of wood, roofed with sods': Clodagh Tait, '"As legacie upon my soule": the wills of the Irish Catholic community, *c*.1550–*c*.1660' in Robert Armstrong and Tadhg Ó hAnnracháin

(eds), *Community in early modern Ireland*
(Dublin, 2006), pp 179–198 at p. 191;
Massari, 'My Irish campaign', p. 248.

12 Casway, 'The Belturbet council and
election of March 1650', pp 160–1,
170; idem, *Owen Roe O'Neill*,
pp 241–64.

13 O'Connell, *The diocese of Kilmore*,
p. 419; Ó hAnnracháin, *Catholic
reformation in Ireland*, p. 50, n. 69.

14 O'Connell, *The diocese of Kilmore*,
p. 419; Manning, 'Clogh Oughter

castle', pp 35–6; Ó Mórdha, 'Hugh
O'Reilly', p. 39.

15 Gilbert (ed.), *A contemporary history of
affairs in Ireland*, iii, 371–5.

16 MacKiernan, 'Thomas Fitzsimons',
pp 315–17; O'Connell, *The diocese of
Kilmore*, pp 429–35, 439.

17 Ford, 'The reformation in Kilmore
before 1641', p. 84.

18 Manning, 'Clogh Oughter castle',
p. 36.